THE AUTOPILOT
MARKETING
PLAYBOOK

10 Proven Strategies to Explode Your Sales

& Dominate Your Local Market

...No Matter How Long You've Been in Business!

CHRIS LOOMIS

For Ian & Alaina,
who inspire me to break through barriers.
I pray I can return the favor.

TABLE OF CONTENTS

INTRODUCTION

You and I are kindred spirits.

You got into business with the goal to have FREEDOM. The freedom to control your narrative, set the tone, and answer to no one. **The kind of freedom that comes with financial abundance.**

This playbook will show you the proven strategies to get there. **But if you continue to do what everyone else is doing, you'll get what everyone else gets.**

Most businesses approach marketing like this: they see someone who has a full-page ad in a local magazine or is on Facebook and think, "It must be working. I need to do that!" So they copy what their competitors are doing without knowing if those ads are really working. The reality is that large sums of money are wasted on terrible and ineffective marketing.

So ask yourself this, if you keep doing what you've been doing, **where will you be a year from now if you don't take action?**

I know because I was there once too. So study these strategies I'm sharing with you. Take them to heart. Implement them and watch the magic unfold!

But before we get into the meat of this book, you're probably wondering who I am and why you should take the time to read and digest the strategies in this book.

Why You Should Read This Book

Let me tell you a quick story about a time when my marketing stunk and what it cost me.

There I was, a new business owner trying to make a go of it. Trying to make a difference in aviation safety by training pilots to be safer and more prepared for emergencies. It was a training program I'd poured my heart and soul into.

I owned an aerobatic, airshow-style airplane (a Pitts S2C for any airplane geeks out there) and installed five video cameras on it, which at the time was something nobody was doing. And this was before GoPros were around!

I measured all kinds of data with the cameras. And because we studied the videos after each flight, we could track measurable deficiencies or gains in improvement and then apply that to the next flight.

It was truly cutting-edge training, but the thing is, at the time I was barely getting by. My wife had to work extra days every month so we could pay the bills. Initially business was slow, and I was struggling to get customers, even though my local competition was busy. At the time it made no sense to me because I had a better training program and a lower price.

But the big problem was that nobody could find me. I didn't have that "place on the busy corner." **And worse, I had no idea how to market my business!** I thought if I just built a website, customers would call me. Boy, was I ever naïve! To start, the problem was I had a website that was horrible, and nobody could find it. And if they did find it, it's doubtful it would convince anyone to call me because I hadn't yet learned the 11 secrets of converting websites that I teach in this book.

So I tried various ad campaigns—including Google Ad Words. That generated some leads, but mostly sucked my money up because I was advertising to a website that was poorly designed and one that made it difficult to convert cold leads.

Then the worst thing happened: the economy started sliding fast (2008) and since my marketing stunk and nobody could find me online, I was unable to make enough money to weather the storm which put me out of business after almost three years.

I became part of that ugly statistic that 50% of businesses fail in the first 5 years. By the way, my biggest competitors survived that recession and are still in business today—**because they had better marketing and were ranked at the top of the search results on Google.**

I was devastated. I started to doubt my ability to run a business. But I didn't give up. I knew I was missing something.

That started my journey into Direct Response and Digital Marketing.

I learned through failure that innovation and hard work alone won't sustain a new company. You also need effective and strategic marketing.

That's when I got serious about learning everything I could about marketing. I became obsessed really, and learned under some of the biggest names in digital marketing.

At that point, everything changed because it all made sense!

I finally figured out how to:

- Model the most successful websites that have been proven to convert.
- Use the 11 secrets of website building to get discovered online.
- Use education-based marketing and funnels to get more sales.
- Leverage the best marketing secrets to grow my business quickly and easily.

Because I learned and mastered these marketing secrets, I was able to:

- Grow my business without going broke.
- Not worry about going out of business again.
- Avoid wasting money on advertising that doesn't convert to sales.
- Help other local business owners grow their businesses faster.

Those years of training and trial and error made it crystal clear to me how to design a website, and marketing strategies that not only get leads and sales but actually run on autopilot. I established that I could not only increase my revenue, but more importantly, protect my company from a slow economy.

I made it my mission to start helping other small business owners like you to avoid failure and struggle by helping you to avoid the mistakes I made.

So I started my own digital marketing company, and this time built a converting WordPress website that Google actually loves. But I didn't stop there.

I then implemented a strategic marketing plan using Search Engine Optimization (getting ranked on Google) and using ads that drive to a lead generation funnel with a specific target audience. The SEO plan got my website ranked on page one of Google in less than 6 months in a VERY COMPETITIVE market, helping to protect me from a downturn in the economy. And the ads-to-funnel allowed me to boost sales and profits—now paying for the SEO.

It worked like magic . . . hence the Autopilot Marketing System.

This is the same approach that I used to help a local painter get more business by building him a converting website and getting his website ranked on page one of Google in less than six months. When I met him, he was placing full-page ads in local magazines that were costing a lot of money with very little return.

Now he is ranked #1 and gets found organically through Google searches and has seen a large increase in business. In fact, he doubled his revenue in less than 9 months . . . and he's been in business for over 15 years!

Building on that success, I decided to create websites and funnels for local businesses to help them generate immediate revenue and get them found online so they can stop surviving and start thriving.

With this book, you will learn 10 strategies to put your marketing on autopilot and dominate the competition:

1) How to get clarity in your business and find your best buyers.
2) How to create irresistible offers.
3) How to use education-based marketing.

4) 11 secrets of a winning website.

5) The power of sales funnels and how to use them.

6) Starting your first Google Ads campaign.

7) Retargeting with Facebook.

8) Do-it-yourself SEO 101 to get your website found online.

9) The power of follow-up with email.

10) How to get more 5-star online reviews.

Ask yourself this, "Where will you be if you don't take this action to invest in your marketing? Will you have met your revenue goals in 12 months or 5 years? Or will you still be where you are today? Will your company be able to handle another recession or the next pandemic? Or will you be out of business and have to go work for someone else who did invest in marketing?"

This can save you from suffering financially or worrying about what you'll do when the economy slides again (like the heartache I went through with my aviation business).

It's a digital marketing plan that can not only help you outlast your competition but also give you the FREEDOM that comes with a successful business.

And that's why I'm so excited to share this information with you so you can get these types of results too!

What this book IS and what this book is NOT

This book is intended to teach you the proven marketing strategies used by thousands of successful businesses. They have been battle-tested and proven to work for businesses of nearly all types and markets.

But there is more to running a successful business than marketing. You also need effective systems, innovation, and cashflow. This book does not dive into those areas of business. This is strictly a book that focuses on marketing strategies for local businesses.

Any results depicted or implied in this book are atypical of most businesses. There are no guarantees or promises that you will have the same results as those described herein. Results can vary depending on your business niche and how well you implement these strategies. Everything provided in this book, all strategies and suggestions, are provided on an "at your own risk" basis.

While results are never guaranteed with any book like this, **your chance of success greatly improves if you take heart, roll up your sleeves, and fully implement the 10 strategies in this book.**

There's a saying that says the best time to plant a shade tree was 20 years ago, but the second-best time is today. So roll your sleeves up, because today we start planting your shade tree.

STRATEGY #1: IT STARTS WITH CLARITY

If there's one subject you will hear all of the business masters repeat, it's that you need to get clarity in your business. You need to dial in who you serve and how you will serve them. You need to define and understand your ideal client on a deep level, understand what their biggest challenges are, and what you can do to solve it better than your competition.

Clarity is like the foundation to a house. If not built correctly, it's something that causes everything else to be out of alignment. Before the house is built, a foundation needs to be level, square, and built on solid ground. Imagine trying to build a house on quicksand. How long before it sinks?

Clarity does several things of great importance in business:

- It will increase your sales.
- It will set your company up for long-term success.
- It helps you narrow down your customer market making it easier to find them.
- It will help you understand your best buyers.
- And it helps you define your purpose.

In this chapter, you will learn 9 steps to gain clarity:

1) Narrow your FOCUS.
2) Define WHO your best buyers are.

3) Define WHERE your best buyers are.
4) Define WHAT drives your best buyers.
5) Answer the question WHY you?
6) Understand your message is not about YOU.
7) Define the LIFETIME VALUE of your customer.
8) Define your BIG WHY.
9) Be the REAL you.

I like to think of clarity as the flight plan you create for your business and life. Ideally, business and personal life blend perfectly and complement one another.

In aviation, for pilots to get from A to B, we create a flight plan. That involves checking all known threats like weather, airspace restrictions, and aircraft limitations. It also includes finding ways to optimize, like finding favorable winds and altitudes for speed and fuel savings.

When you have a flight plan to get to where you want to go, you're not going in blind. You suddenly have focus and clarity.

Most people when starting a small local business do one of two things. They either just print up some cheap business cards, maybe some fliers, and start spreading the word on social media hoping for some business or they obsess over logos and things that don't bring in immediate income. Of the two, the first is a better option in my opinion. At least you are putting in place some marketing that will get you income now.

But wouldn't it be nice to have a flight plan with goals and focused steps to not only get your business started with making money now but also give you the clarity to achieve your end goal or dream?

That's the power of clarity and why I think it is the most important and powerful strategy in this book. Let's start building your flight plan.

STEP 1 – Narrow Your Focus

There's a saying that says, "The riches are in the niches."

Take that statement to heart, because it's been proven by thousands of successful businesses. If you aren't convinced, just look at the medical profession. How much do you pay an orthopedic surgeon versus a general practitioner? And guess what, their pay is commiserated with their skill and education.

If you had a dog that has accidents in the house, who would you hire? Would you choose a run-of-the-mill dog trainer or a dog trainer who specializes in helping with dog accidents? Are you willing to save a little money and hire someone who just trains dogs to sit, speak, and obey your commands OR are you willing to pay a little more and hire someone who specializes in stopping dog accidents while you're away, especially if they guarantee results?

People who have a specific concern or need are often willing to pay more to solve that problem or need.

As entrepreneurs and business owners, we naturally want to get all the business we can and think we should market to everybody. But the harsh reality is that under normal circumstances, only about 1–5% of ads convert to sales. That means that you are throwing 95–99% of your ad spend away!

So you're better off focusing on a target market where you will have a more interested group of people who are looking for what you are offering.

The majority of businesses miss the mark on this. They go for the shotgun approach. They go a mile wide, but it only goes an inch deep. **You need to think differently and go an inch wide and a mile deep.**

Would you rather hire a handyman to pour your custom stamped concrete patio or an experienced concrete professional? Or better yet, would you rather hire a concrete professional who SPECIALIZES in custom stamped concrete?

While both concrete contractors might be able to perform that work equally well, the contractor who positions and markets as a specialist is targeting a specific client and need. And because of it, they will have a better positioning.

If you own a home service business, such as a painting company for example, and you were looking to invest in marketing to help you get more clients, would you rather hire a marketing company that specializes and has success in helping services business owners and contractors like you reach more clients at higher prices or hire the big marketing firm who claims they do it all for everyone?

By narrowing your focus, you will be able to charge more for your services as those prospects will only want to work with you because you have positioned yourself as the expert who can solve their problem or need.

Meanwhile, most of your competitors are all trying to market to everyone, slamming every social media site with terrible "look at me" spam ads. I'm willing to bet they are all competing on lowest or best price using those techniques. **And since there can only be one lowest priced service provider, it's literally a race to the bottom.** That's not a place you want to be!

One of the big mistakes small business owners make is to try to attract everyone to buy their products or services. It's natural to want to attract everyone, thinking you need to spread the word as far as possible.

We see big companies on TV and on radio and think I need to copy them. Of course, most small businesses could not even come close to affording that type of advertising, but furthermore, it's not the type of advertising you want anyway.

That's brand advertising and these companies spend huge amounts of money to get you to see their ads over and over and over, hoping that when you do need insurance or a pizza you'd call them first. It's risky and very expensive.

When you're small, you need to think targeted advertising. While it would be awesome if everyone was interested, the truth is that very few are interested in what you are selling. Normal marketing returns see only 1–5% of prospects buy! That's a lot of wasted marketing dollars if you ask me.

A way to lower your marketing ad spend or to convert a higher percentage of prospects to buyers is to define your best buyer avatar, or your "Who." Your best buyer avatar is a detailed representation of your typical or ideal client.

If you do this correctly you could see returns of 50% of the people you target could be interested, especially if you use a low-cost entry or education-based marketing.

STEP 2 – Define WHO Your Best Buyers Are

You may have heard of the 80/20 rule.

It was created by an Italian economist named Vilfredo Pareto in 1895. Essentially, he determined that 80% of results come from 20% of the effort. He determined that at the time in Italy, 80% of the land was owned by 20% of the population.

But the interesting thing about Pareto's Principle is that it has been proven to apply to many aspects of business. **A well-known axiom in business is that 80% of sales come from 20% of the customers.**

That last statement should get you excited! Because knowledge in business is power and if you know who your 20% is, you can go find more of those types of dream clients to dramatically increase your sales.

It's worth repeating that huge sums of money are wasted on marketing by businesses every year. This is because 80% of business owners market to 80% of the people. **In other words, they market to everybody instead of narrowing their focus to attract the 20% who bring them 80% of their sales.**

But on the flip side, the businesses that dominate (the 20%) understand the 80/20 rule and market to their 'bread-and-butter' type of dream clients. This all makes more sense when you consider 80% of businesses fail or struggle and only 20% thrive.

Start paying attention to the flyers, mailers, and local magazines that come to your mailbox. Take a few minutes each day to analyze these ads. You'll likely find that 80% of them all are positioning and marketing themselves in a very similar way.

They will talk about their experience or expertise. They will have a picture of themselves or their business. They will say, "Call us, we can help" or something along those lines. Eighty percent of ads are puffery or boasting their business without proof, without a compelling offer that has a very specific and defined benefit.

Eighty percent of ads won't have spoken to the client. They will not have gotten their attention with a good headline or image that implies they have something urgent and important to share, something the prospect must stop and listen to. **They will not have an offer or a reason for a prospect to call them today.**

Most of the ads you see are filled with fluff and words that WILL NOT convert to sales, because they do not motivate a prospect to contact you. In fact, this serious problem bleeds over into other forms of media like their website, Facebook profiles and social media posts.

If you're thinking, "Crap, I do this!" Please don't worry. By the end of this chapter, you will have learned how to fix that, how to find your ideal client, and how to get into the 20% of businesses that thrive!

An important point on determining your WHO: your best buyer is NOT YOU! I'll say it again, because it's that important. **You are not your best buyer!** To find and further define your best buyer, you'll need to start with learning their demographics and psychographics.

STEP 3 – Define WHERE They Live and Hang out Online

Once you know WHO your dream client is, we can use that information to find and target them using demographics and psychographics. Once you understand how to use these two powerful tools you will be able to find your dream client online.

Demographics

You are probably familiar with demographics. It includes things like age, gender, race, income, marital status, location such as what neighborhood they live in, etc.

To find your best buyers, you need to first ask some specific questions to define them so you can locate them.

What is their income level? Are they men or women? What neighborhood do you want to work in if you're someone like a painter or landscaper? Those questions are the start to defining your best buyer.

Let's say you are a restaurant owner (but this can work for any business). Maybe you find that your best buyer is men, ages 40–65, high-income professionals with home values of $500k+, and who live in a specific part of town, maybe a 5–10 mile radius. Imagine having that information! You could now target those neighborhoods to get more similar clients.

And in light of the COVID-19 pandemic, you can use this to your advantage. There's a restaurant my wife and I love, but the restaurant is 45 minutes south of where we live. Their entire menu is composed of gluten-free foods. It's hard to find gluten-free restaurants, especially ones that are really good.

That restaurant not only has unbelievable food, but they understand their customer avatar. They know where their best buyers come from and have started offering online ordering of meals-to-go, delivered to a drop-off point in our area. Sure, it's a bit of a drive for the restaurant, but because they had this data they can pivot and serve and keep money coming in while many other restaurants are closed during the pandemic.

Psychographics

Psychographics is where you go deeper into the mind of your client. Demographics explain who your 20% is while psychographics explains why they buy. Psychographics include similarities in lifestyle, activities, interests, attitudes, and aspirations.

Let's take a closer look at each of these.

Lifestyle

Lifestyle might be something like healthy eating, exercise, or hosting dinner parties because of one's profession. Maybe you find that many of your clients love to host parties at their homes. This is knowledge you can use to understand what they want and what they worry about. Certainly, they want to impress their guests. And maybe they worry about sitting space, or decorations and tapestries being outdated. If you are an interior designer, you'd be able to speak directly to that person by talking about the impact the right space can have on the overall vibe of the evening and in making their guests walk away saying, "Wow!"

Activities

Activities are their hobbies. Let's pretend you own a company that sells high-end tailored suits delivered to your client's office or home. If you find many of your clients are into sports cars, you could then craft a marketing message that compares your suits to a high-end sports car by implying that they would get the same confidence and sense of power with your suits as by driving that sports car. Using a language your avatar instantly identifies with is very powerful. Because suddenly they feel like you get them and are speaking directly to them.

Interests

Interests signify things your client avatar likes to enjoy. For example, let's say you run a fitness program. And let's assume you've dialed in your demographics and your program is geared towards men. Now if you find out your clients are married men with children, you know one of their interests is family life and balancing that with fitness. That changes how you speak to them. It would be different than talking to the 22-year-old new professional who's single. If you create a program designed to help these dads gain maximum results with their body while increasing TIME and ENGAGEMENT at home, you not only have a niche offer, you have a hungry audience. And you'd likely have supportive spouses for their husband's time away.

Attitudes

Attitudes would be things like opinions on politics. For example, an interesting niche at the moment is conservatives who like patriotic gear such as t-shirts and hats. It's a very specific audience, but they are passionate about supporting that cause. So if you owned a restaurant where the majority of your customers were conservatives, it would be easier to create offers and messaging that speaks to that prospect.

Aspirations

Aspirations are your customers' dreams and might be the most powerful of the psychographic marketing tools. This is where you look closely at who your best buyer really is and what keeps them up at night. This is powerful when it concerns what you sell, because **you need to understand that people aren't buying a service or product just to have a service or product.** They want to know what that product or service will do for them, what it will help them achieve or eliminate. That could be things like confidence, health, memories, comfort, or trust.

For example, if you are a dentist you're not just selling clean teeth and veneers, you are selling confidence. People want to have a smile they feel confident about. While they want white straight teeth, what they really want is how that makes them feel. So when you know this, your messaging changes. They aren't buying veneers because they want veneers, they are buying what the veneers will give them.

If you can connect with a prospect emotionally, you will have an advantage over your competition. No doubt you'll have better marketing and better odds of getting them to call you or come into your shop.

How to Use Demographics and Psychographics

If you already have a client base, you can use surveys to gather this information. You can simply ask them in normal conversation. You can use invoices to see what part of town they live in and map out where your top 20% live so you can target more of the same clients through direct mail (which by the way is far from dead!).

So if you know that a majority of your target audience lives in XYZ neighborhoods, then this is a great place to start your mail campaign. Rather than sending mailers to an entire city or zip code, focus instead on certain neighborhoods. If your avatar is high income, you can target neighborhoods with high home values.

As far as finding them online, demographics works great with Facebook. This is not a lesson on how to set up all of those campaigns—as that is a lesson by itself—but I will give you some examples of why it works and what to do to get started.

Facebook is one of the most powerful marketing tools out there. But just a quick note on that: if your target audience doesn't use Facebook, this is not going to work to attract them. You want to go where they are hanging out. It could be LinkedIn, Instagram, or maybe it's just through Google searches and Google Ads.

But Facebook is a great tool, because when you boost a post or run a Facebook retargeting ad, it allows you to segment who you target based on age, gender, location by zip code, or city (more on this in strategy 6).

Facebook knows this based on someone's profile, what they typically buy, what they 'like', etcetera. It's actually kind of scary what Facebook knows about us, but knowing that they have this information on us, gives you an advantage in targeting your best buyers!

Psychographics is the bread and butter of targeting. It's even more powerful than demographics because you can target people who have certain beliefs, who follow certain people, or who have specific buying patterns.

You can use psychographics in social media (again Facebook is super powerful for this), use it on your website and with your Google campaigns.

With Facebook, when you boost a post or create an ad, not only can you target the demographics we discussed above, but you can target things that they might be interested in or people they follow. For example, if you know your dream client likes or drives luxury cars, you can easily target them by telling Facebook to find people who like BMW or Mercedes. If someone has liked a BMW, or commented on BMWs, posted pictures of BMWs, Facebook will know and be able to target them for you. Using that along with the demographics of where they live can be super powerful for you when targeting local markets.

If your best buyers like or follow famous personalities, TV shows, podcasts, musicians, golfers, then you can target them too.

Psychographics makes marketing incredibly targeted

When you learn where your best buyers live, what they do for a living, and other demographics, and then learn their psychographics, you will have an edge over your competition. If you've done your research correctly, you will nail some of these. And when you start speaking to them in your copy, social media posts, and videos they will think you know them personally and are talking directly to them. That's powerful stuff and you will convert more leads to sales—guaranteed.

STEP 4 – Define WHAT Drives Them

People don't buy from you because they understand you, they buy from you because they feel understood. Do you understand the slight difference? You need to get inside your best buyer's head if you want them to understand you.

Let's say you are a guitar teacher and wanted to target musicians for lessons, you'd not only want to know who they are and where to find them, but equally important is what to say. This is one thing many business owners miss the mark on, and it will cost you sales!

Don't talk in a language that they don't understand. For example, you might ask, "Are you having trouble with your hammer-ons and pull-offs? Would you like to know how the pros use the simple pentatonic blues scale in these top 100 rock songs?"

If you used that language, you'd be targeting a very specific type of student and excluding others. Clearly, it wouldn't be a beginner. You'd be targeting someone who is past learning how to tune a guitar. They probably know a good many chords and even a handful of songs already. Now if instead you talked about tuning guitars, bar chords, or music theory, you'd be targeting a completely different avatar! This is why it's critical you understand your WHO.

So you can see how the language you use will attract a specific type of client. Famous marketer Richard Collier said you need to enter the conversation already happening in your prospect's mind.

Here are some questions you can ask to help get into your prospect's mind:

What keeps them up at night? What's your avatar's biggest source of pain? What are they struggling with? What are they fearful of? What's their biggest problem that they don't even see yet that you can speak to them about in your ads, website, social media, and emails?

You also want to consider their greatest opportunities. What are they really trying to achieve? What are their hopes and dreams? Who or what do they aspire to be? (This may not be applicable, depending on what you sell).

Take a few minutes and brainstorm and answer these questions. What did you learn about your best buyer that you didn't already know?

Your advertising and social media copy should use terms and language that your dream client identifies with and connects to. This gets them emotionally engaged and helps you connect with them on a level that not only they like and understand, but on a level with which they identify. People prefer to do business with like-minded people, not people they have nothing in common with.

To find the language they use, if you don't already know it, you can join a Facebook group where they hang out and listen to what they say. You can go into forums or Google groups (groups.google.com).

Not only will you learn the language people use, but you'll also likely find out what their biggest and most urgent problems are! What keeps them up at night? What are they really trying to achieve? People are always asking for help in groups. Not only do they tell you what they need help with, they also give you clues as to how you should craft your sales messages, website, and SEO keywords!

STEP 5 – Answer the Question, "WHY YOU?"

To answer that question: you need to develop a USP!

The Unique Selling Proposition, or USP, was created by marketing genius Rosser Reeves, and he discusses this method in his book,

Reality in Marketing. It is a method that has since been used by many of the best marketers over the years and by some of the biggest brands you are familiar with:

- Like Geico Insurance's "15 minutes can save you 15% or more,"
- Or Domino's Pizza "Get fresh, hot pizza delivered to your doorstep in 30 minutes or it's free,"
- And FedEx's USP was, "When you absolutely, positively must have it tomorrow, ship it FedEx."

This is a huge component of effective marketing and not enough businesses use this. If your ads aren't converting well, or if your revenue is less than you anticipated, then getting a USP will change both of those! It's something that will take a little work and time in developing or dialing in, but when done, will bring you in more revenue.

So how do you develop a USP? To get the gist of it, you need to answer these questions to start: Why should anyone buy your product or service versus your competitors? What's makes your business, product, or service different or unique?

Dan Kennedy, in his book *Magnetic Marketing*, says that to find your USP, you need to be able to answer the question, "Why should I choose you versus any provider of the same service or product that others provide?"

Here's a quick exercise that can help you answer that question.

In one minute or less, tell me what it is about your business that gives you an advantage, benefits your clients, or gets better results for your clients than your competition.

The answer I normally see and hear is, "I've been in business for X years." And "I have low prices" or "The best service in town" or the ever popular "We take our work seriously." Doesn't everyone?

None of those are a USP. None of those will separate you from your competitors, because likely they are saying the same things and are not unique.

If you owned a dog training business, you could use something like this: "Good dog guaranteed. We stop your dog from peeing in the house in 30 days." That is an example of an effective USP, (and is actually a real USP for a dog training business). It instantly and succinctly tells you what they do and how it benefits their dream client and target niche—people looking to stop their dogs from having accidents inside the house.

Here's another example. "Fix it free forever if the fix fails." That is a USP of an auto mechanic repair shop. What they are saying is if after we fix your car, that car part or issue is guaranteed by us for life. That USP will make a lot of people feel good buying—knowing that they are protected—but it also does something different. What it also does is help to build trust in the prospect's mind, which is a big deal in that industry where many auto mechanic shops are not trusted 100%.

You could claim to be "The most highly reviewed business in your niche in town," and that's a good USP also. It's effective because it shows longevity and shows social proof that people are happy with your business, service, or product.

It's important to know that people do not buy products or services because they want that product or service. They buy because of the benefits or results it will provide. When you hire an HVAC company to replace your AC unit, you don't hire them because you want a new AC unit, you hire them because you want reliable cold air in the summer and heat in the winter from a company you can trust.

And sometimes your product or service is a function of emotion, like buying a car. People don't buy a sports car because it goes fast, they buy it because of how it makes them feel when they drive it.

You wouldn't buy a drill because of its specs: 1.3 battery amp hours, 15 clutch settings, quick connection drill bits, and an ergonomic handle when all the drills in the store taut the same specs. You buy it because you need a hole drilled and that drill gets great reviews on reliability, has the lowest price, or has the best package of components with it. You're buying the benefits, not the features. **Understanding that distinction is critical to creating a USP and Offer that converts into sales as opposed to one that doesn't.**

Rosser Reeves says the USP will have 3 parts:

1) It must make a specific proposition. Not just words or bragging. But more along the lines of "Buy this and you will get this benefit."
2) The offer must be unique. It must be something that the competition either does not offer or cannot offer or claim.
3) Uniqueness is not enough. The proposition must be so strong that it will entice new buyers to purchase.

Now you may be wondering, what if you have a very similar service or product to your competition? How do you distinguish yourself? Well, there are a few ways.

First, you could work on improving your product or service so that it offers a unique benefit. Maybe that is using pet and child-friendly green products if you own a cleaning company. Maybe that's guaranteeing results in six months if you own an agency. Maybe you ensure the concrete you pour is cured properly by sealing it for free, no matter how big or small the job. Or maybe it's a friendly welcome and smiling customer service every time a customer visits your business.

Have you ever been to Disney? They claim it's "The happiest place on Earth." And they mean it. My wife and I have been to Disney with our kids many times, and I'm always amazed at how the staff is always smiling and helpful. They take their USP to heart and deliver on it.

Southwest Airlines states their USP clearly on the homepage of their website: "Why fly Southwest? No change fees. We never charge a fee to change your flight." When most every other airline nickels-and-dimes you with fees, Southwest does it differently.

If we can learn from those who have paved the way before us, we can achieve success faster.

The second way to distinguish your product or service is to **add value to your service or product.** You can create a tower offer and add massive value. I talk more about this and how to create it in Strategy 2.

A third way to distinguish your business is to reveal something about your service or product that is relatively unknown to your prospects. A good way to do this is through education-based marketing, where you describe the benefit of working with you over others by simply educating them on your service. I go more in-depth on this in Strategy 3.

Bottom line, take time to figure out what makes your business, service, or product unique. Then put that into a simple and succinct message on your website, social media, and ads that propels your dream clients to choose you versus the competition.

If you do nothing else in this book, do this!

STEP 6 – Understand HOW to Talk to Your WHO

How many times have your eyes glazed over when you sat and suffered through talking with someone at work or a lunch meeting who only drones on and on about themselves? Never giving you a chance to chime in. Or if you do get a quick chance, you are quickly "one-upped" with a better story. The talented comedian Brian Regan refers to this as the "Me Monster."

To me, these people can be tough to be around. They seem to have zero self-awareness. And they don't seem to care about you.

But sadly, you see this in businesses more often than not. Everyone wants to brag or boast about their service, skills, or experience without first trying to get to know the client or asking them some questions that might get them thinking about something that maybe they didn't even realize they might need.

For example, you'd never walk up to someone at Starbucks and just start talking about how great you are, how much money you make, awards you've won in your business . . . would you? No. You'd lose somebody before you even finished your breath.

But that's just how most business websites, ads, and messages are built. As soon as the home page loads you're bombarded with talk of how great they are, how long they've been in business, all of the awards they claim, even if it's 8 years ago! It's all about them.

You'll have better success if you can listen first. Try to understand your prospect's pain points and challenges. Once you convey that you know and understand them, have a solution for them, THEN you can go on to talk about your experience, awards and showcase your testimonials.

For example, imagine you own a landscaping company, and rather than having your marketing materials always shouting about how great you are, if instead you asked a simple question, "Are you tired of having the ugliest yard on the street?"

"Do you want grass that stays green and lush throughout the year?"

"Is your to-do list overwhelming you?"

"Do you want a landscaper who doesn't push you off for a week because they are 'backed up?'

Depending on your best buyer (and if you've done your homework you now know them better), you've now talked directly to their pain points. If they can answer yes to one of those, you have their attention. Then you can introduce your service, product, or solution to them. Once you've done that, jump in and tell them why you are the one to help, present your irresistible offer, and showcase your testimonials.

The main takeaway here is to remember whenever you write copy for your website, landing page, email, print ads, social media, videos, you need to speak to the best buyer you are targeting. Speak to their pain points, their desires, and less about you. This all starts with listening to them.

If you are going to talk about you, use stories. Everyone loves a good story. And it's more engaging than just stating facts.

STEP 7 – Determine the LIFETIME VALUE of Your Best Buyer

First, let's start with defining what the Lifetime Value of a Customer means and why you need to know this. The Lifetime Value (LTV) is the average dollar amount a customer is worth over the life of your business.

So many businesses don't know this number and will have an arbitrary marketing budget, never really knowing what they can spend and what it costs to acquire that customer or lead. sep

Stop looking at overall marketing budgets, like you have 1k per month to spend. Instead, look at your budget per lead or per sale. If you know your LTV, and what your conversion rate is on leads, you know what you can spend to acquire a new customer and remain profitable.

Let's use the example of a realtor. Assume the average home value in your area is $500,000. If you make 3% commission on the sale of that loan, your cut is $15,000. After you give your broker 30%, you keep $10,500.

So if you never listed or sold a home for that client again, the average lifetime value of a customer is $10,500. And if you managed to get repeat clients say 1 out of 10, that number would be a little higher yet.

But let's assume your LTV is $10,500. That means you can spend $10,500 on advertising to acquire that customer and you'll still break even. That's powerful information! Once you know this number, you now have a real operating budget for your marketing.

Let's look at another example. You may remember a product called ICY HOT. It was a cream that helped alleviate the pain of arthritis and sore muscles. It sold for $3 for a jar.

Jay Abraham, a genius marketing guru was the brains behind the company's wild success. He went to all media outlets, magazines, newspapers, radio, and said if you run an ad for the product, anyone who buys through your ad, you keep the $3 for each jar sold through that ad! All he asked was they send him the name and address of each customer so he could follow up and ensure they were happy and got the product. (That process is actually far easier today through your online sales funnels.)

Jay knew the lifetime value was that the customer would buy 10 more jars each year, and they'd buy directly from the website or through his email campaigns to them.

This created an unlimited budget because he only paid for sales. He built that company from 20k to 13 million in 18 months!

You can get creative like Jay did and come up with an affiliate or commission-based offer. If you know the LTV of your customer, it might make sense to pay your salesman 100% commission on the first sale. They'd be working much harder to get that sale for you. **If you have a business that gets repeat customers, understand that your current customer is worth 10–15x more than a prospect.**

Here's how to determine the LTV of your customer:

1) Average worst-case unit sale customer is worth (not best case).
2) How many times they'll buy from you in the first year.
3) How many years they'll be with you.

Something that goes hand in hand with LTV is a low entry offer. This is something very attractive to your prospect that costs them very little. It could be only $1.

If you owned an auto repair shop, and you had an offer that your first oil change was only $1, that's an offer that's pretty darn irresistible. But at only $1 for an oil change, you'd lose money on that service . . . so why would anyone do that?! Well, if you know the LTV of your customer is say $2,000, it would make a lot of sense to get them in the door to give you a try. Losing a little money on the first low entry offer is a no-brainer now.

When you know your LTV, and you combine that with an irresistible low entry offer, you now have the beginning of a marketing system that will run for you on autopilot.

STEP 8 – Define Your BIG WHY

You might be wondering why something like a "Big Why" matters. It's not a trivial subject. It's actually one of the more important topics in this book, because along the way of building a successful business you're going to hit many roadblocks, detours, and speed bumps. And when you have your Big Why at the forefront of your thought, you will have better odds of persevering.

If you've ever been through a personal development or business coaching program—such as those from Tony Robbins to Dean Graziosi to Jeff Walker—you will hear them continually go back to your Big Why.

They don't necessarily call it that. They might talk about what drives you, what's your purpose, what gets you out of bed in the morning excited, etc. These are all the same concepts.

Now I'm not some motivational guru or personal development coach, so I'm not going to pretend to be one, but I do want to hammer home this one very important thing: **you absolutely need to define why you want to own and/or run your business.**

There's a reason these coaches all focus their business coaching programs around personal development. **Because it all revolves around you and what you bring to the business.** If you are carrying around stress, lack passion, or have chaos in your personal life, what do you think your business will turn into?

Here's a great exercise to get to the heart of your Big Why. It's called 7 Levels Deep. It's something I learned from Dean Graziosi in his coaching program, "Knowledge Broker Blueprint." You can also learn more about this in his book, *Millionaire Success Habits*.

It's a really powerful exercise and it will definitely get you thinking differently. It will give you purpose in your business as it relates to your life. Not only can it help you get through the tough times, but it's something you can use as daily motivation.

Here's how it works.

I want you to get some paper and a pen. Don't go any further until you have that, because this is an exercise, and if you don't write it down, it won't really work.

Got paper and pen? Okay. So I'm going to ask you seven questions and I want you to write down the answer. Don't overthink it. Just write down what comes to you and what's in your gut. What's yelling at you telling you to listen. This won't work unless you write it down!

7 Level Deep Exercise:

- Question 1: Why did you buy this book?
- Question 2: Why is it important for you to (answer to question 1)? For example, if you answered question one by saying, "You bought this book so you could learn about marketing for your business." Then question 2 will ask, "Why is it important for you to want to learn about marketing for your business?"
- Question 3: Why is it important for you to (answer to question 2)? You will repeat this for 7 questions. Not 6, not 8—it's 7 questions! Don't ask why, but just trust me on this and after you answer these seven questions you will know your Big Why.
- Question 4: Why is it important for you to (answer to question 3)?

- Question 5: Why is it important for you to (answer to question 4)?
- Question 6: Why is it important for you to (answer to question 5)?
- Question 7: Why is it important for you to (answer to question 6)?

So did you find your Big Why? Pretty awesome, right? For me, this simple exercise really created a big mental shift. I have a really awesome and high paying job as an airline pilot, a successful digital marketing company, and when writing this book, I needed to define my Big Why. Because I didn't really *need* to do this. Financially, I was already set. But something was pulling at me. In the end, my Big Why wasn't what I expected it to be.

Now obviously, some of my initial reasons for writing this book are to help other entrepreneurs succeed quicker and avoid the pain of closing a business like I had to endure. And I also would like to make a profit out of the deal. Those are all expected reasons. But after answering all 7 questions, my final answer hit me like a punch in the gut. It wasn't about making money. It wasn't about success. My deepest level wasn't even about my kids who I thought for sure it would be about. **It was about having choices and being able to control my destiny without relying on a paycheck from someone else.**

It's knowing your Big Why that will give you an edge over your competition, but you now have real skin in the game, not just a few bucks and time.

So the next time you wonder why you're getting up early to head to a job site that's less than desirable, or having difficulties with an employee, or maybe just having an off day, just go back to your 7 Levels Deep and remember why you're doing this in the first place.

STEP 9 – Be the REAL You

If you haven't made any enemies in business, then you aren't working hard enough to separate yourself from the pack. When you have enemies, you'll have achieved success on a new level. You have become unafraid to stand for what you believe in and are willing to take the heat. When you have enemies, it means you are making an impact on your community and not caving to appease others because your success doesn't seem fair.

It doesn't mean you cheat and lie. In fact, it's just the opposite. The jealous types will always be enemies of the businessmen and women who run their business with integrity, never caving to media or social standards, all while leading the way in their niche market.

Thing is, if you're afraid to anger someone or make them jealous, it's likely not your fault. As children, we are taught to avoid conflict at all costs. We are taught to feel bad for those who aren't as good as us at something. I guess winning hurts feelings, so now participation trophies are handed out just for showing up. What a joke!

How is the kid who is proud of a participation trophy going to fare as an entrepreneur when it's dog-eat-dog? Probably not as well as the kid who had to experience the pain and heartache of losing but also got to experience the thrill of winning and has a trophy because they worked for it.

Those kids are more likely to be the lion and not the gazelle.

The second point I want to make, and this is important, don't let anyone make you feel bad for being competitive. Don't let anyone make you feel bad for what you stand for. Because I promise you will have critics. The jealous will rear their heads and maybe take cheap shots on social media or yelp or wherever they think they can inflict damage.

As long as you run your business with integrity and are following your heart in what you stand for, you will continue to be successful.

The best example of doubling down on what you stand for is Chick-fil-A. They make no apologies for being closed on Sundays to observe the Sabbath Day. They get mud slung at them daily, but in the process, they have grown a huge following and monster business with excellent customer service.

If you've ever been through a Chick-fil-A drive-through line, you know what I mean. There's never NOT a long line.

My challenge to you is to stand for something you believe in. You might be surprised how many people will identify with what you stand for or at least love that you do have the confidence to stand for something. And if you always make it a point to serve your customers at the highest level, you will have greater odds of success.

We aren't taught to go in for the kill. But that's how you need to think in business. You need to go for the jugular like a lion.

That doesn't mean you are trying to destroy your competition by attacking them. It's a metaphor for having the lion inside you to strive to dominate. You need to run your business like you want to be the go-to place. In fact, you should feel bad for those who purchase your competitors' products or services.

Thing is, you can have this competitive drive, stand for something, and still be humble. You can be the lion and still have a big heart.

This is a topic that not only is frequently overlooked, but also something many businesses shy away from for fear of being criticized or losing business. It's standing for something meaningful to you, and being unafraid to make it public—no matter if it means you'll be criticized.

STRATEGY #2: CREATE AN IRRESISTIBLE OFFER

I think this is a concept that you can identify with because nearly everyone has experienced the power and persuasion of a really good offer. You've seen them on TV, in clothing stores, used in service businesses, etc. In fact, you might have bought something that you didn't even need and thought . . . wow, how did that happen?!

That's the power of a really good offer. And when you combine that to a targeted audience, someone who is in need of what you have to sell, it's very powerful and you'll convert at a much higher percentage. **AND if done correctly, at a higher price.**

Most businesses all market the same. They all scream "Buy from me! I have the lowest price!" Or they claim to be the best. But either way, they just want you to buy now. But the problem is they are missing two key things:

1) They don't have a no-brainer, low-risk and low-cost offer, and

2) They don't have an irresistible higher-end offer with a high perceived value.

According to Jay Abraham, the brilliant marketer, there are three ways to grow your business:

1) Increase the number of customers and clients who purchase from you.

2) Increase the unit of sale (higher price and profit margins).

3) Increase the frequency of purchase per each customer.

Now if you just do any one of these, you will grow your business geometrically. Do any two and you will grow exponentially. Most people only think of increasing number one. Do all three by 10% and you increase your overall revenue by 30%!

There are two techniques in creating an offer that you can use to increase these metrics. Both types of offers must be irresistible. The first one I like to use is an easy, low-risk, low-cost entry offer. The second type of offer is to use what's called a tower offer.

Use a low-price entry offer to boost Jay Abraham's #1 and #3, the number of clients who purchase and the frequency of purchase. Use the tower offer to increase #2, higher prices and profit margins.

Let's take a closer look at each of these powerful strategies.

Low-risk, Low-cost Offer

Most business owners copy other business owners' marketing. The problem with that is that most marketing stinks! So if you copy them, odds are that you'll get what they get: high ad costs with low return on investment.

So if you want to lower your ad spend, you need to increase your lead conversions. A very effective way to do this is to have a low-risk, low-cost offer. Let's look at a few examples.

This is a really good example of a low-cost irresistible offer. Only $1 for your first oil change is a no-brainer and as low-cost as you can get without the offer being free. Plus they offer a $25 Visa gift card. That makes it very irresistible.

Maybe you're wondering why they would do this or even how they can afford it? The answer to both of those questions goes back to Strategy 1 where we covered the Lifetime Value of a Customer.

This auto repair shop understands the average LTV of their customers. They know that if they can get someone to come in for a $1 oil change, and if they do a great job servicing that vehicle, there's a pretty good chance that they will come back for more oil changes, PLUS when they need something repaired, who do you think they're going to call?

If I owned an auto repair shop, this would be one of the best ways to attract new clients who will continue to come back to see me. You could make it so the offer is only valid for new cars (not new owners) or make the offer valid for a limited time.

Let's look at another example:

This is a men's hair cut salon. Not only are they unique because it's more of a membership club, but also have a unique experience in the lounge as well. To get men to try it out, they have a no-brainer low-risk, low-cost offer for $1 for your first haircut. Now are they losing money on the first haircut? Sure. But again, they understand that if they over-deliver and knock it out of the park, that $1 first haircut will turn into hundreds of dollars per year (or more) per client.

This method of creating a low-risk, low-cost offer should be readily visible on the home page of your website. This is the place where new visitors can learn about what makes you unique and why they should consider your business. Having the low-entry offer can help push them over from a researching prospect to a new customer.

But what if you don't have a business model where you have low-cost offers already? Well, you could offer free consultations. You'd have to spell out what's included and why it's of high value. I use this in my own agency business. We put together a marketing plan tailored for local businesses to help them explode their sales. It includes things like a website evaluation, keyword research, spying on competitors, and ideas for a low-cost offer for their business. And it's free.

You may have to experiment with various offers to see what works best. But once you find it, it will work like magic to help you bring in new customers that are searching for your service.

The Tower Offer

Remember those old commercials for OxiClean? Billy Mays delivered a great pitch! But the offer is what got people to buy and sell millions of dollars of OxiClean.

https://youtu.be/ZTpXh33Mbeg

First, he tells you all about the 'benefits' of OxiClean. Notice he doesn't tell you the features, like what it's made of. They understood that people don't buy features. They buy the benefits.

He tells you it works on carpeting, laundry, whites, and brights. It doesn't ruin fabric like bleach. After he gets you all excited, he has an Irresistible Offer for you. You get a 2.5-pound tub of OxiClean today for $19.95 (normally $40). Plus he gives you the squirt bottle and Super Shammy for FREE. If you call now you get a bottle of the OxiClean Orange Clean. And if you call in the next 20 minutes, he will triple size your OxiClean tub from 2.5 pounds to 6 pounds! But that extra bonus is only available for the next 20 minutes.

So here's what you get for $19.95:

- 6-Pound tub of OxiClean
- Squirt Bottle
- Super Shammy
- OxiClean Orange Clean

That's a pretty good deal. They knew that offers sell better than plain old products.

Imagine trying to sell just the one 2.5-pound tub of OxiClean for the discounted price of $19.95. That's a half-off price and still a good deal, right? But with that offer, there's no way they could have done near the sales they did. The tower offer is what pushes people over the edge of indecision.

The single product offer is how most businesses make offers. They come up with a discounted price and hope it will create a large volume of sales. But the better way is to create a tower offer, stacking multiple products or services on top of one another—similar to what OxiClean did.

Ideally, your offer value is about 10X the value of the original stand-alone product. There are a lot of ways to do this that won't cost you very much off your bottom line. And if you understand the lifetime value of your customers, you know what you can offer. A great additional resource on this topic is Russell Brunson's book *Expert Secrets*.

Here are some ideas on creating an irresistible offer using the tower offer:

- Offer more of the same product.
- Offer free supplement products that go with the original offer.
- Free swag, like hats and t-shirts.
- Free how-to training guide.
- Free training videos.

- Free eBook or audiobook.
- Pay-in-full discount.
- Add in an additional service that is of high perceived value but easy and affordable for you to do.
- With extra things that you normally include, break these out as bonuses with tangible values.
- Create an ultimate package offer.

Part two of an irresistible offer is SCARCITY. People naturally procrastinate. To motivate people to buy now, you need to add in scarcity. You can do this a couple of ways. Either have a deadline where the offer expires and is no longer available or offer a limited amount.

But here's the thing. You have to stick to it. You can't keep opening the offer back up after you close it down, or people will be on to you and it won't convert as well.

If you want to keep the offer up longer, you can introduce scarcity by removing some of the bonuses after a certain timeline or after so many offers have been purchased. But anytime you create an irresistible tower offer, you must have some type of scarcity to motivate the prospect.

As an example, if I was a landscaper, I'd create an offer for the beginning of each season. Either limit the time available or only take a limited number of projects. I'm not a landscaper and don't have a green thumb, so if you do, don't judge this offer. I'm making this up on the fly.

Before you create the offer, I'm assuming of course that you've gotten clarity and know WHO your best buyer is, WHERE they live, and WHAT challenges they are facing. One example of an offer might be for spring. You could offer a landscape make-over package. Include 6 15-gallon bushes planted for X price, maybe $1,500–$2,000 (depending on where you live and what the bushes are would change the price). Some ideas on things you could include for free: plant fertilizer, pruning shears, gardening gloves, lawn aeration and seeding, spring leaf clean up, or tree pruning.

You wouldn't have to include all of those, just enough stuff to motivate the prospects to secure their spot. The cool thing with online sales funnels is you can split test the offers to see which convert better.

So now it's your turn. Start brainstorming and create as many bonuses to your service as you can think of. Don't worry about what it costs at this point. Just go for the wow factor. Think only about how cool, over-the-top and irresistible you can make it. Then, you can reshape it to something that works in your business while still maintaining profits.

STRATEGY #3: USE EDUCATION-BASED MARKETING

Education-based marketing might be the most under-utilized method of lead generation for local businesses. It can be just as powerful as reviews and testimonials. The thing I like about education-based marketing is that it is a great way to introduce a new prospect or cold lead to who you are and what you do. It can build trust and likability.

When someone is searching for a product or a service, and they come across your website that has free educational information for them, there's a good chance that they are going to listen to what you have to say—especially if you get the headline right.

For example, if you were looking to have a concrete driveway poured, you'd likely start by doing a Google search for concrete contractors in your area. **First, we know that most buyers don't go past the first page of search results which is why investing in SEO is one of the single best investments a local business can make in their marketing.**

After Googling concrete contractor imagine seeing a search result that has one of these headlines, "Avoid the Costly Mistake of Hiring the Wrong Concrete Contractor" or "How to Have Your Concrete Poured Properly at the Best Possible Price."

Would you be interested to see what it has to say? Well if you're looking to have your concrete done properly at the best price, you're likely going to see what this is about. After clicking on the link, you see a landing page (simple website page) that has a headline and a video.

The headline says, "Learn the 5 Shortcuts Many Concrete Contractors Take That Can Weaken and Ruin Your Concrete."

The video goes on to educate you about slump. Slump is essentially the amount of water that is added to concrete. The higher the slump, the more water is in the mix. The more water that's in the mix, the weaker the concrete. The ideal slump is between 4 inches and 5 inches.

Concrete is heavy. It's 6,000 pounds per cubic yard. And the concrete workers don't like to pull and push concrete too much because it's hard on the back. So one shortcut they take is telling the concrete driver to add more water to the mix putting the concrete at a 7–8" slump. What this does is make the concrete more self-leveling. Genius, right?

The mix comes out of the truck easier and the workers barely have to push or pull the heavy concrete. Then they screed it level and finish it. The problem with that is all of that extra water really weakens the concrete and can cause extra cracking, dusting, and popping, among other issues.

The video would go on to explain the other four cheats that concrete guys take that you didn't know about. So now that you know the shortcuts and rip-offs some companies take, who are you going to call to have your concrete work done? Add in some great testimonials to the page, an irresistible offer, and it's conversion magic.

That's the power of education-based marketing. It doesn't work for every business, but if you can find a way to educate your buyers, do it. Even if you're giving away your secrets, it's okay. It's not like your competition is going to copy your video and message. Likely, they won't even know where to start with something like that.

Education-based marketing gives you an advantage over your competitors. It also allows you to stop competing on price. A good strategy is to point your direct mail ads to this piece of educational information.

I learned this strategy from Joe Polish, who used it to scale his carpet cleaning business. At the time he started using this strategy he had an automated phone line to call to get the information. Nowadays the preferred method is to use landing pages and videos. But a recorded phone message could still work, depending on the niche.

Joe's headline read, "How to Get Your Carpets Cleaned Properly at the Lowest Possible Price." Once they got on the free call, they would learn, "7 Questions to Ask a Carpet Cleaner Before You Invite Him into Your Home, 6 Costly Misconceptions About Carpet Cleaning, 8 Mistakes to Avoid When Choosing a Carpet Cleaner, and How to Avoid the 4 Carpet Cleaning Rip-offs!"

Joe used this strategy to help him take his carpet cleaning business from broke to a million-dollar business, eventually creating the "Rich Cleaner System" to help other carpet cleaners scale their businesses.

So not only does education-based marketing educate the buyer, it makes you look smart and trustworthy. This falls into what Robert Cialdini calls Reciprocity. Because you are giving away such great and useful information for free, people naturally want to give back. They do that by buying your service or product, or maybe just by referring you.

Let's look at another really good example of education-based marketing, this one for a product. Have you ever heard of the Sleep Number Bed? Well if you Google that, you'll see the competitors' ads. One of them is the Personal Comfort Bed.

They have an ad that says, "Sleep Number Bed vs Personal Comfort|50% Off Closeout." That ad takes you to a landing page that compares the two beds, and you see right away how superior Personal Comfort is over Sleep Number, and for a lot less cost to you.

Furthermore, their landing page is very well laid out. It states very clearly what makes them different, then takes you right into the education-based video. As you scroll down the page you learn more about the benefits of the bed, more side-by-side comparisons, video testimonials, and thousands of user testimonials.

https://www.personalcomfortbed.com/

So whether you have a service-based business or you sell a product, hopefully, you can see from these examples that using an education-based marketing video can really help win new customers with trust and expertise.

I use education-based marketing in my own marketing campaigns. In fact, you might be reading this book as a result of watching one of the videos I have that talks about one of the 10 strategies in my Autopilot Marketing System.

So I am challenging you to brainstorm some ideas on information that you can give away for free that would help your prospects make better decisions. Notice I didn't say help make you more money or help get them to buy from you. Sure, in the end, that's what we want as business owners, but that should not be your focus when creating education-based marketing. Think only of your prospect and how you can help them.

You want to create something of high value that your prospects will find very useful to help them make better buying decisions. When the information is so good that even your competition wants more of your free information, you know you've got a winner!

STRATEGY #4: 11 SECRETS OF A WINNING WEBSITE

I'm always amazed at how many small businesses don't have a website. I see these businesses try to rely on print marketing (usually with very low conversions because there's no offer) or they rely strictly on social media, which is just rented space with algorithms that restrict how much you are seen unless you pay big money for ads.

Any business that relies solely on one avenue for marketing can get into trouble. You want to invest in a minimum of two mediums, ideally a short-term lead generator and a long-term lead generator. For example, your short-term lead generator could be Facebook or Print Ads. Your long-term lead generator should be a properly built website with SEO.

A website is the digital front door to your business. It is one of the single most powerful marketing tools when done correctly. Of course, on the flip side, if done incorrectly, it's not only a large waste of money, but it can cost you lost revenue because it's as bad as not having a website at all.

By having a website, it allows the prospect to investigate and see who you are and how you can help solve their problem. That's the key. It's you telling them how they can benefit by calling you or doing business with you.

A website has several objectives, depending on what you sell.

- Allow prospects to learn about your company and how you can help them.
- Find your company online which lends to legitimacy.
- Allow you to craft sales offers and sell products.
- A place to capture leads via email or phone calls.
- Showcase testimonials, case studies, and social proof.

If you use the following 11 website secrets your website will become a money converting machine for your business:

SECRET #1 – Use a WordPress platform to build your website on. No HTML. No monthly subscription platforms, unless it's built on WordPress. My favorite is DropFunnels.

SECRET #2 – Make sure your website is mobile-friendly.

SECRET #3 – Ensure your website is geared for speed. Your home page should load in 4 seconds or less if possible.

SECRET #4 – Make sure your website uses original copy. Google knows when you use duplicate copy from other sites and will penalize your rankings if you do.

SECRET #5 – Avoid bad neighbors by investing in secure and fast hosting.

SECRET #6 – Get your website secured with SSL.

SECRET #7 – Use high-quality images. Buy high-quality stock photos and/or have a professional photographer take some photos of you and your team.

SECRET #8 – Put your USP on your homepage so prospects know why they should choose you.

SECRET #9 – Collect leads via email or text capture with Free Reports, Coupons, or Education-Based Marketing.

SECRET #10 – Display testimonials and reviews on your home page and sales funnels.

SECRET #11 – Optimize your homepage with on-page SEO

In this section I will go more in-depth on the 11 website secrets and why you need to follow these if you want your website to collect leads and get prospects to call you, buy from you, or visit your shop. If you are able to get all 11 of these website secrets right, you will have a big advantage over your competitors. Odds are they won't have even half of these secrets right which means your website will more easily rank to the top of Google search results. And when a prospect actually does click on your site, you've got your message and offer dialed in so that it motivates your prospects to action.

So let's go under the hood and look more closely at each of these 11 website secrets.

SECRET #1 – Use WordPress to Build Your Website

WordPress is the most popular platform used for websites worldwide. Roughly 50% of all websites are built using WordPress. So there are many advantages to those numbers. For one, Google loves WordPress. And two, it will be much easier to find a designer to help you build your website or fix it if needed. And three, they are totally customizable with hundreds of add-on options.

What you want to avoid is an HTML (coded) website. Unless you have a large complex business (think FedEx or Target), you don't need HTML. In fact, HTML will cost you a lot of money to have someone fix or adjust the website. And it could be difficult to find someone other than the person or company who built it due to the unique coding the designer may have used.

I once had a guy want to build me a website using HTML and he said it had 11 languages of code so it would be super secure. Thing is, it's no more secure than a WordPress site. Many large corporations use WordPress, including the media giant Disney. So WordPress is equally secure.

WordPress is also the most flexible platform due to the hundreds of plugins you can use. Plugins are like apps on an iPhone or iPad. They integrate with your website giving you endless options for customization. We use plugins to compress images, speed up websites, add pop-ups for your offers, integrate bookings, display Google reviews, and integrate with sales funnel software. The options are truly endless and it's getting better all of the time.

So avoid HTML sites because they are expensive and cumbersome. And I also recommend avoiding non-WordPress monthly subscription platforms to use as your main website. There is a mountain of articles that mention that these types of platforms are not as Google-friendly when it comes to SEO as WordPress sites. Sure, they're attractive with a low entry cost, but I find WordPress sites easier to rank on Google. Plus you have limited functionality when it comes to plugins and integrations with most subscription platforms.

The exception to monthly subscription platforms is DropFunnels. I use this for my own site actually. It's super powerful, lightning-fast, totally customizable, and my favorite platform for building websites and funnels. And DropFunnels uses WordPress.

SECRET #2 – Make Sure Your Website is Mobile-Friendly

It probably goes without saying that more and more people every day are searching for things on their smartphones. It is estimated that over 50% of all searches online are done with mobile phones, and that number will only continue to rise.

This is why it's so important that your site is mobile-friendly. But what does that mean . . . to be mobile-friendly?

It means that your website when viewed on a mobile phone or iPad loads properly. There should not be random text missing, hiding, or half off of the page.

All images should be centered or appropriate for the message. Often, I'll remove an image and just use a solid background for a section if the image doesn't fit properly or looks awkward.

The site should flow naturally for scrolling. So one-page sites with minimal clicking work well for this. You can still have other supporting pages for your services but having the critical information on the home page helps keeps a prospect from leaving your page in frustration.

Also, you want to have a clickable phone number or Google map, depending on what you want the prospect to do. Both of these should be very easy to find.

Take the mobile-friendly test: https://search.google.com/test/mobile-friendly

And since so many searches are done on mobile phones, often without WIFI and just cell service, leads to the next secret: Speed.

SECRET #3 – Ensure Your Website is Geared for Speed

This is one of the secrets that you really must try to get right. A slow-loading website has several consequences.

First, Google will penalize you for a slow-loading site. It will be very difficult to rank a slow website high on Google search results.

Secondly, it makes for a terrible user experience. We live in a nanosecond culture. People get frustrated waiting for a fast-food cheeseburger these days. They will not have much patience if your site is taking forever to load.

They will just 'bounce' and proceed to your competitor's website.

You should be shooting for an initial load time of 4 seconds or less for your home page. That holds true for your sales pages as well. Your advertising costs will be lower with faster load times.

If you have an image gallery, this would be the one exception to that. People expect those pages to load a little slower. If you have a ton of images, consider breaking them up into multiple pages directed by a menu.

Use www.gtmetrix.com to check load times.

TIP: Use Cloudflare as a Content Delivery Network (CDN). It's free and integrates with most hosting. It basically speeds your site up as requests come in from different parts of the country or world.

SECRET #4 – Make Sure Your Website Uses Original Copy

This might seem obvious, but maybe you're wondering why it matters? Who cares if you copy content from someone else's site that maybe explains your services, right?

Wrong!

Google knows when you use duplicate content from other sites and WILL penalize your rankings if you do it. I actually tested this out with one of my older sites.

I bought a whitepaper a couple of years ago, a book that I have legal rights to use as my own. It was a short but decent book on SEO marketing. So I thought, cool. I can give this away to anyone who visits my site . . . or I can use the contents of the chapters as blog posts.

Knowing that I wasn't the only one who was using the book, I was risking my rankings but I wanted to test it.

So I published a couple of blog pages with the content from the book. I checked www.copyscape.com to see if the content existed in other places, and it did —many places actually.

But I left the content up to see what would happen. About two weeks after I posted it, my rankings began to fall. At the time I was ranked at #7 on page one for SEO Services in my city. After about four weeks, I had fallen to page 3.

And rankings won't come back quickly once Google slaps you with this penalty!

So be sure to use only original copy. **Do not fall for the temptation to use someone else's words from their site. You will pay dearly for it!**

SECRET #5 – Use Secure and Fast Hosting

Most people can comprehend websites and why some are better than others. But hosting is something that confuses most people when they are first researching and trying to figure out how to get a website up.

In layman's terms, hosting is simply a place on a server where your website lives. All of the images, content, videos, etc. need memory. It needs to be stored somewhere. The hosting company is the place where all of that is stored.

Normally, how this works is hosting companies have various plans you can choose from, depending on the traffic you have and the speed you want. Remember, you always want speed as this is very important to Google and to users.

The hosting companies sell these plans, and then put you on a 'shared server.' You can get dedicated servers, but these are very expensive and not necessary for most companies.

But it is important to be on a server that has good neighbors. Getting on the wrong server would be like buying a house in a bad part of town. You'd be at risk. Well, your website would be at risk if you share server space with sites that promote or sell adult content, gambling, and some Pharma products.

So how do you know? Well, for starters most hosting companies won't tell you who you share your server space with. But you can check it out for yourself by visiting this site:

www.viewdns.info/reverseip

Or you can use our hosting, which never allows bad neighbors. This way you never have to worry. We also restrict the number of websites per server which helps with speed.

The cheaper hosting plans will typically have more bad neighbors and these cheaper plans also fill up their servers to maximum capacity which slows down your site. So I recommend going with a business hosting account.

You also want a CDN, also known as a Content Delivery Network. A CDN is a group of servers strategically placed that communicate with your hosting server to increase load times and provide additional layers of security.

Cloudflare is who I use for my own site and my clients. This is a free service, so making the decision to add this is a no-brainer.

One last note about bad neighbors. If you use hosting that allows this (most do), and you happen to see a couple of bad neighbors, don't be alarmed. According to Google, a couple of them won't hurt your rankings, but when you start to see quite a few on the same server as yours, it's time to switch.

Lastly, the hosting companies have security measures to protect your site from hackers (often free). That leads us to Secret 6.

SECRET #6 – Get Your Website Secured With SSL

SSL, or Security Sockets Layer, is a protocol that ensures data sent via the internet is private and secure by using encryption. You know a website is secure and using SSL when you see the padlock symbol in the browser.

🔒 https://autopilotmarketing.io

Most hosting companies offer SSL as part of their plans. Business plans usually offer this as a free add-on service.

Your site should start with https://. The "s" at the end of http means it is secure. If you don't see this, contact your hosting company and have them add SSL.

Why is SSL so important?

- It's going to be very hard to get your website ranked on Google without it. Google puts a lot of weight on SSL.
- SSL websites are prioritized in search results. So if your site doesn't have SSL and your competitors do, you'll be swimming upstream to get on the first page of search results.
- It's a red flag for most prospects. They won't want to give you any information, not even on a contact form, without knowing their information is safe.

SECRET #7 – Use High-Quality Images

How many websites have you seen—and I was guilty of this once upon a time too—where the website just has a lot of very poor-quality photos? It's actually pretty common, but it sends a message to your customer that you aren't a professional.

It's kind of like showing up to a meeting or presentation in shorts, flip flops and an old t-shirt. Unless you're a guru teaching someone how to surf or kiteboard, it wouldn't send a good first impression. You need to think of your website in the same way.

You need to capture the attention of your prospect. High-quality images—no matter what industry you are in—will give you higher marks.

Here's what I recommend:

- Hire a photographer to do professional headshots and transparent background shots. This allows you to put your image in various places and blend it in naturally with your theme colors without the distraction of a noisy background.
- Get high-quality images related to your services. Action photos are good. There are many places online that offer high-quality stock photos.
- Use images that evoke emotion. Remember that people buy with emotion and justify the purchase with logic. Compelling imagery along with a compelling headline is powerful. This goes back to knowing your avatar, what their desires are and what they want to avoid.

There are exceptions to using non-professional photos. For example, you might have some good photos of you that highlight your experience. As long as it ties into what you do, it can work.

For example, I have a picture on my 'About' page of me in the cockpit of a Boeing 777. It gives a little peek inside of who I am and my journey. People who read about me know I've been flying airplanes since 1991. And it ties into my marketing agency because it was in my aviation business where I first learned that **effective marketing matters.**

So feel free to use some personal photos (higher quality of course) that might help to tell a story. Otherwise, if you want your website to look professional and awesome, you should use only professional or high-quality stock images.

SECRET #8 – Put Your USP on Your Homepage

We talked earlier about the USP and why it's important. You don't want to be the one with the website that repeatedly beats its chest like a gorilla on how good you are. There is a way to do that subtly by showing where you've been featured, your online reviews, video testimonials (covered in strategy 10).

When someone clicks on your website, they should be able to quickly learn why they should choose you. Remember, this isn't because you claim to be the best, or because you're really good at something. This is your Big Promise.

A good place to put your USP is either right at the top of your site above the fold as a heading or in your Why Choose Us section. Either way, it needs to be on your home page and prominent to help prospects make the decision to choose you.

SECRET #9 – Use Direct Response Marketing

As discussed in Strategy 2 on Irresistible Offers, direct response marketing is an age-old method of marketing and still works awesome today! If you are not using this, you are missing out on more leads and sales. You absolutely need to be using this marketing strategy if you want to sell more or sell at a higher price.

You can deploy education-based marketing on your website in the form of video or sales copy. You can and should be using it in your funnels. You need to give people a reason to respond, click, or call now.

Maybe you have a coupon that is only good this week. Or a limited time offer. Or an education-based video explaining how to hire your service for the best price done properly by exposing the shortcuts and cheats other businesses use that you don't. Then you move them into your low-entry, no-brainer offer.

The cool thing about using direct response marketing in your funnels is that you can split test various strategies. In other words, every other time someone clicks on your landing page, a different headline or offer is displayed. You keep testing until you have a winner and then you can test that against another headline or offer until you have your winning formula. Then you just let it run on autopilot!

SECRET #10 – Display Reviews on Your Homepage and Funnels

I know this might seem obvious, but so many sites lack this important feature! How often have you read reviews on Amazon or other places before buying? I know I do.

So if you can display your Google reviews right on your home page, maybe in a scrolling banner, it's pretty powerful. Or my favorite, to add video reviews. Those can be even better. And when used in conjunction with Google reviews, it can motivate prospects into your buying circle.

Video reviews work really well on your sales funnels. This is the page where you have one specific product or service for sale (and hopefully you have created an irresistible offer!). As prospects are reading about your service or product, they see your great offer but maybe they are still unsure. Video testimonials from past customers help give you social proof that you deliver on your big promise.

SECRET #11 – Optimize Your Homepage and Funnels with On-Page SEO

Essentially, if you want your website to get found on Google, you need to make sure it's Google compliant. In other words, Google recognizes it and likes it.

To do this, in addition to the above website secrets, you need to take the time to update your website on-page SEO. These include things like image optimization, Alt Tags, Heading Tags, Keywords and Metadata.

If you don't do this, your website isn't going to be seen by anyone unless you send them there directly. It won't be found with Google searches. It's kind of like having your signage behind trees and your building tucked way back behind everyone making it impossible to get drive-by traffic. No one is going to find you unless you direct them there.

I cover on-page SEO in more detail in Strategy 8.

STRATEGY #5: USE LANDING PAGES AND SALES FUNNELS

A landing page is basically a simple webpage with an offer and is normally NOT the main home page for a business. Think of it as a "side door" to your website.

It typically has no header or menu, and no sidebar ads. It usually has just one offer for a target audience. **The reason you only have one offer or action is because a confused mind will take no action.**

Have you ever seen a kid in the candy aisle trying to choose a candy? There are so many options and colors, they don't know what to choose! It's not much different for adults either. Maybe not the candy aisle, but for so many other things we shop for we are indecisive and hold off on the purchase. I'm sure you can relate.

The beautiful thing about a landing page is that there is only ONE option. That could be to book a consultation or schedule an appointment. It could be to 'opt-in' to their email list by downloading a free guide or book. It could be to buy a particular product. It could be to try your fitness program for free on a trial basis. The options and uses of landing pages are limitless.

The main point of a landing page is to get a prospect to do ONE THING and one thing only. There's no menu because you don't want them leaving the page. The landing page is where they go after they've read a blog post or Facebook post and you grabbed their interest for something you offer.

The Sales Funnel

A sales funnel is similar to a landing page, except you have a sequence of pages that connect to one another in a certain order.

A funnel has three components. It starts with a landing page. Often the landing page will have a simple opt-in, like a free guide or free training video. But it could be your low-cost irresistible offer as well.

Once prospects opt in, it takes them to a new page with your main offer. This would be your main sales page.

If they buy that offer, the next page might be a one-time up-sell offer—only available right then and there. That offer could be a complimentary service or product, or more of the same product. The one-time offer page is optional.

The last page will be a thank you page, which may also explain what to do next. Here is a visual representation of a simple 4-step funnel.

Funnel Steps

Opt-in Page → Sales Page → One-time Offer Page → Thank You Page

A good website will have a clear call to action on the homepage. Here's an example of a sales funnel for a fitness gym I stumbled across while doing research.

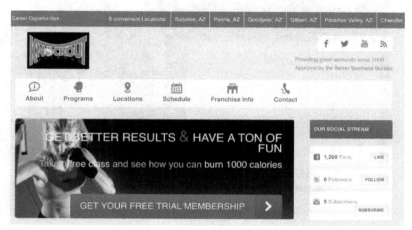

www.knockout-fitness.com

They are a gym for women in Arizona that focuses on kickboxing training. On the homepage is a clear call to action to sign up for a free trial where you'll burn 1000 calories per workout.

Click on the offer and you are taken to a landing page where you have to opt in with name and email to get the free pass. https://knockout-fitness.com/landing-page-1/

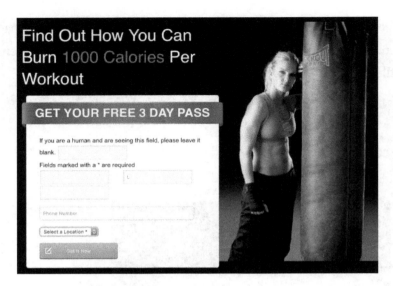

Once you opt in you are taken to a thank you page where you get a coupon code to bring for your free sessions. http://knockout-fitness.com/thank-you

It's a very simple funnel, but the headline and imagery are compelling, and the offer is good. Your funnel doesn't need to be complex. It just has to have a compelling headline and offer.

NOTE: A few critiques on this funnel are that they don't use and SSL on some pages (https) and you always make sure your URL slug describes what the page is about. You don't want it to be /landing-page. Instead, it should be something like /free-trial.

Once you have the funnel built, you'll want to send all ads and social media to the landing page (not the homepage of your website). Remember, you want to eliminate confusion and overwhelm. Give your prospects only one option, one thing to do.

The great thing about these landing pages is that they are so easy to split test. You can test headlines, colors, fonts, and offers.

The landing page should have a simple offer. It could be a training video and a downloadable work-out plan or meal plan if you provide your email.

Once you opt in, you would be taken to a sales page, listing all of the benefits of the training program and gym, video testimonials from members, and an offer to join the gym. In addition, there might be several bonuses you'd get for signing up. The bonuses expire and there is a count-down timer showing you the urgency needed to grab it now before it's gone.

If they take the offer, they are taken to a checkout page and then to a thank you page with any instructions you may need to give them.

When you advertise on social media or Google, you should send your ads to the landing page. Try focusing on getting leads versus the sale now. The great thing about a well-designed funnel is that you can actually get both. You will have those who opt in to get your free expert guide, but do not purchase your product or service. That's okay. Because now you have their email or phone number and can follow up with them. Not everyone is ready to buy from you this instant. In fact, only 3% of buyers are ready to buy right away. That's still a great number and you want to attract that buyer. A good funnel can really boost your sales due to its flexibility and conversion.

The others who aren't ready yet, some will be in a few months. The great news is that you have their email address and now can continue to add more value by email. And you can follow up with more offers later (more on this in Strategy 9).

Landing Page and Funnel Software

There are several really great options out there with which to build your landing pages and funnels. The three I'm listing here, I've used them all extensively. This is not meant to be a user review, simply a resource for you so that you have a good place to start.

DropFunnels – www.dropfunnels.com. ($49 per month)

DropFunnels is my favorite landing page and funnel builder. It is fairly new to the market at the time of this writing. They have fast and great customer support via their Facebook page. And they are coming out with new features each week.

Biggest Benefits:

- Lightning-fast load times.
- 100% built with WordPress.
- Use for your main website PLUS use for landing pages and funnels!
- Easiest editor of the 3 options.
- Includes hosting for your website.
- Built-in Blog feature made for SEO and getting your site found online organically.
- Great price at $49/month.

ClickFunnels – www.clickfunnels.com ($97–$297 per month)

ClickFunnels has been around since 2016 and has a huge fan base. I've built funnels with their software for myself and my clients.

Biggest Benefits:

- Incredible training options.
- Integrates seamlessly with your WordPress site as a plugin.
- Easy site builder.
- Nice templates.
- Self-hosted.
- Lots of funnel options, like quiz funnels, product funnels, service funnels, membership funnels, etc.

Leadpages – www.leadpages.net ($39 per month)

Leadpages is not really a funnel builder as much as a landing page builder. But they do a great job at making high converting landing pages. If all you need is a simple landing page, this is the best option.

Biggest Benefits:

- Good-looking landing pages.
- Fast load times.
- Tons of templates.
- Good training.
- Affordable if all you need is a landing page.
- Integrates with WordPress with a plugin.

STRATEGY #6: USE GOOGLE ADS

There are customers searching for your services every day on Google. **What would it be worth to you to have your website found in the top of the search results?** The best option is to have your site ranked and found organically through SEO, but that is a long-term process. It's worth every effort and dollar spent but expect it to take six months to get your website there.

In the meantime, you should be using Google ads to place your website and offers at the top of the search results. There are two ways to do this. And several reasons why you should implement both of these strategies.

First, you should set up an ad that uses your brand and company name as the keyword. This will likely cost you very little per month. No one will see this ad unless they search for your company. If you don't have much of a presence online or are just getting started in business, it won't cost much. As you gain a bigger presence online and become more well-known, people will start searching for your company and it will start performing.

To recap:

- The focus keyword will be your company name.
- Point the ad to your main website.
- In the description describe what you do, what services you offer, and add your phone number.

The second type of ad you should run is for the irresistible offer we talked about in strategy #2. Most ads you see point to their main page. That converts poorly. Most people are going to ignore those ads, to begin with, especially if it's a basic ad to a website.

You want the ad to point to your sales funnel landing page, that's the page where your offer lives. The reason for this is because you want whoever clicks on your ad to have only one thing to do, one action to take. That could be to call you. It could be to buy your offer online. It could be to opt in for your coupon or free guide. **Either way, you want them to take action!**

Since they are actively searching for your services, you use those keywords as focus for the ad. So, for example, if someone searches for "Dog Potty Training near me," I'd want to advertise that business with an ad that targets that long-tail keyword.

The way you don't want to do it is to have your ad very general. Here's an example of what I mean:

dog potty training near me   ✕ 🎤 🔍

🔍 All   🛒 Shopping   📍 Maps   📰 News   ▶ Videos   ⋮ More   Settings   Tools

About 71,500,000 results (0.90 seconds)

Ad · www.olk9tn.dog/ ▾   (877) 758-2404
Aggression Experts - Private & 2-Week Board & Train - olk9tn.dog
Join Our Pack Today! Set Your **Dog** Up For Success With Off-Leash K9 **Trainers**. Fast Response. Solve Your **Dog's** Nipping, Biting, Pulling & Jumping Problems. Basic or Advanced Obedience. Therapy **Dog Training**. All Breeds, Ages & Issues. 2 Week Board & Train.
📍 **509 Memorial Blvd, Murfreesboro, TN** - Hours & services may vary

This ad might work if the prospect was searching for a dog trainer to help with aggression. The ad needs to address what the prospect is searching for. And for that ad to convert, it needs to point to the landing page with the offer, not your homepage like the ad above.

Here's how I would set it up:

Ad - www.ok9tn.dog/stop-dog-accidents 877-758-2404
We Stop Dog Accidents – Guaranteed! Try Us for Just $1
Are you ready to get your sanity back? We can fix 95% of all dog accident problems. Results guaranteed or your money back. FIRST SESSION JUST $1. Slots are limited. Book now to get on the schedule before we fill up!

Which ad would you click on if you were looking for help with stopping your dog from having accidents in the house? The more targeted your ad is the better it will convert. You need to think about how you can get your prospects, the people searching for your services, to stop dead in their tracks and click on your ad.

STRATEGY #7:
RETARGETING

The next step after setting up your Google ads is to retarget. This technique can be used with several different mediums, such as more Google ads, YouTube ads, Twitter, and Facebook. While all have their benefits, in this book I'm going to talk about Facebook retargeting.

I prefer to use several different mediums in marketing. It's the 'Be Everywhere" thought process. At the time of this writing, Facebook has over 2 billion users, and growing.

Plus Facebook has some of the best marketing tools available.

I do admit that what Facebook knows about us is scary and invasive. They collect hundreds of data points on us. They might know more about us than our closest friends and family do. Not much is secret with them.

But for business owners, this is a goldmine marketing tool you can use to learn more about your customers, their pains, desires, searches, and retarget them. Here's how that works.

When a customer clicks on your website—whether that be because they clicked on a paid ad, your site was found through Google searches and SEO, or because you or someone directed them there—their information is captured by something called a pixel.

This pixel basically grabs their Facebook information, and the next time they go to Facebook they will see your Facebook ad in their feed! I'm sure you've seen this in your own Facebook feed before. Powerful, right?

People will think your ads are everywhere! But in reality, they are the only ones seeing it . . . well them and all of the others who have engaged with your website or other ads.

Personally, I've bought several things from being retargeted. I visited a website and did some research, left, and a few days later I'm still seeing that company's ads. The good ones continue to educate and build authority, but that's an entirely separate topic.

The beautiful thing about retargeting is that you are showing ads to people who now are aware of who you are, and are aware that they have a problem, and that you have a solution to that problem. That's the magic of retargeting.

When you advertise on Facebook to cold traffic, most of the people you target won't know you and may not know they even have a problem. So for those campaigns, you need a different headline and sales copy.

Here are the steps you need to take to set up Facebook retargeting. This is not for cold traffic. That would be a separate ad you would need because your audience would not know you, know you have a solution, and they may not even know they have a problem. So this is just for retargeting an audience of people who are familiar with you, your product, or service (called a warm audience).

How to Set Up Your Facebook Retargeting

1) Install your Facebook pixel on every page of your website. The ideal place is the header. WordPress sites make this pretty easy. DropFunnels, my preferred choice of WordPress platforms, has a separate location to put this so all of your pages are set up with one click.

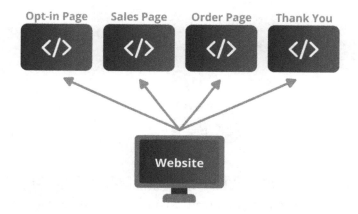

2) Install a different pixel for your thank you page. You want to retarget people who have opted in or purchased from you differently than those who land on your site but don't take those actions. Think back to messaging and getting in the head of your buyers. Your message and ad should be different for each of these if you want to maximize your conversions and minimize your ad spend.

3) Ad Facebook Pixel Helper to your Chrome browser. This is the easiest way to ensure your pixel is firing and working properly. It's free.
https://chrome.google.com/webstore/detail/facebook-pixel-helper/fdgfkebogiimcoedlicjlajpkdmockpc?hl=en

4) Create your Facebook event, called a campaign. This is your objective and where you tell Facebook what action is needed for targeting. Things like they visited your website, they viewed a video, they opted into your email list, they got to your checkout page but didn't purchase (big one!).

5) Create your custom audiences for retargeting, called Adsets. This is where you create an audience that has viewed your website in the last 30 days (hot buyer). For local businesses, you can bump this up to 60 to 90 days. This means that if someone visits your website, they will see your Facebook ads in their feed for that amount of time. You can also retarget based on the % of videos watched, by targeting your email list, followers, visitors to your Instagram page, opened but didn't submit a form, etc. There are many more options.

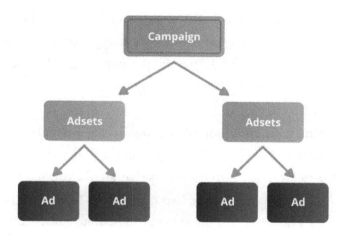

6) Spy on competitors or other successful marketers with a free Facebook tool. See how they set up their ads and use them as a model. http://www.facebook.com/ads/library

7) Build your first Facebook ad. Before you get started, be sure to research what Facebook requires and what they won't approve. They are pretty picky about what you need to do as far as requirements with images, contacts, offers, etc. No more than 20% of text on your image.

8) Create a really catchy headline. This is more important than even the image you use. You want a headline that will stop people in their tracks. Go back to your best buyers and what they are trying to avoid at all costs, and what they truly desire. Create a headline based on those emotional qualities and your ad will convert better.

9) Create the text description. You can use the text on your sales funnel. This way you are testing your sales funnel copy at the same time. If they aren't clicking on your ad to move

to the sales funnel after engaging, it's possible the copy is not converting—so this is a good opportunity to change it.

10) Set your budget. $10–$100 per day is a good place to start, depending on what you are trying to achieve, your budget, etc.

11) Run your Facebook retargeting Ad for 4 days before you change ANYTHING, including the dollar amount.

12) After 4 days, drop the adsets that aren't working from the campaign. And create two more adsets similar to the adsets that do work. Adsets are your look-alike audiences.

13) Continue this process until you have a high-performing winner and then continue to test it by split-testing the headlines.

STRATEGY #8: SEO IS KING

Buyers are searching Google every day for your products and services. **What is it costing you to NOT be at the top of the Google search results?** Many of these are HOT buyers, ready to buy what you offer now, or in the next 30–90 days.

In my opinion, aside from having clarity in your business, being at the top of local Google search results is the single best marketing investment you can make, and it will give you the biggest return on your investment.

Think about it. If you had to hire a plumber for a water leak, what would you do? Most people are going to google "emergency plumber" in their city, or something like that. They aren't going to search Facebook, or LinkedIn, or Instagram. Those platforms are not meant for that.

Imagine owning the plumbing company whose website showed up in the top of the search results for "emergency plumber." What would that do for your business?!

Why Google?

Why not Yahoo or Bing? It's because Google dominates the online search engine traffic. More than 90% of all searches occur on Google, which is why you need to have your business show up there. Yahoo and Bing account for less than 5% combined. In fact, the second biggest search engine is YouTube, and it's owned by Google!

Why page one?

What's wrong with page two? If you want people to click on your website and check out your business, you certainly need to be on page one of Google. **90% of buyers won't go past page one and 70% of buyers won't scroll past the top 4 search results!** Think of that.

How hard is this?

I'm going to break this down step-by-step and show you exactly what I do to get my clients listed at the top of Google. **It's actually much easier than you think!** It just takes diligence and managed expectation.

Keep in mind, large volumes of books have been written on this, so this chapter could easily be a book in and of itself. I'm not going to bore you with the anatomy of search engines and all that. While some of that stuff is interesting, it's not knowledge you require to get found online.

How long does it take?

Google won't put you at the top of search results in 6 weeks no matter how many backlinks and how much content you have. It has to be grown slowly over time and organically.

Depending on your competition, and if you follow the steps in the strategy, you can get there in about 6 months. But don't worry. It's not difficult. It just takes time, patience, and some good old fashioned elbow grease.

But before I get into the nitty-gritty, we need to cover a few important terms so you can follow along more easily. I promise this isn't that technical! I'm no computer whiz and I definitely can't do code. This will be no problem for you! **I am going to break this down so it is easy!**

KEY TERMS

1) **Search Engine Results:** These are the website listings that Google spits out after you type in a keyword or phrase.

2) **Short-tail Keyword:** This is the actual thing you are searching for. For example, if you type in "plumber" it will pull up listings for plumbers, plus it may pull up articles on plumbers, plumber schools, etc. That's because it's a very general search keyword, also called a short-tail keyword. When you add in your city along with it, Google now knows you are looking for plumbing services in your area and it will list for you the top websites for plumbers in your area. It doesn't mean these are the best plumbers, of course, it just means Google finds their website to be the most compliant with Google to be ranked.

3) **Long-tail Keyword:** This is how most people search for something. They type in a phrase. It might be something like, "how to fix a water leak under your sink," or "how to get my dog to stop peeing in the house." It is easier to rank for long-tail keywords than short-tail.

4) **Search Engine Optimization (SEO):** This is the term we use to describe the process of getting your website found in search engines. There are many things that go into it. Google uses hundreds of algorithms to rank a website, and nobody knows what they all are. But we do know there are certain things we can do to increase our odds of winning the ranking game.

5) **On-page SEO:** This is how your main pages are set up to be Google compliant along with keywords on the page.

6) **Off-page SEO:** There are two components to this: backlinks and content.

7) **Backlinks:** A backlink is when another website links to your website.

8) **H1 Title Tags:** Title tags are the headings in your content on the page. You will normally see H1, H2, H3 titles. You only want one H1 Title tag per page, and it should be unique from every other H1 title tag on your website.

9) **Alt Text:** These are the descriptions for your images. They should describe what the image represents so when people do a Google search it can be recognized and show up in their search results.

10) **Meta Title:** This is the heading you see in the search results. Each page of your website should have a unique meta title. It is recommended to keep it at 70 characters.

11) **Meta Description:** This is the description of that web page. It should have the keywords on the webpage in the description and the meta title. It is recommended to keep it at 160 characters.

12) **Slug:** This is the extension on the end of your website page.

13) **Anchor Text:** When you create links to other pages of your websites or other websites, your links should be readable text for Google. Don't use CLICK HERE. Use the actual word. Here's what I mean. How not to do it: "To learn more about Chris Loomis, CLICK HERE." How you should do

it: "Learn more about CHRIS LOOMIS." The anchor text should be the name, highlighted with a different color font.

14) **XML Sitemap:** This is very important to have if you want Google to actually index your website. Most SEO plugins can set this up automatically. It is basically a map of all of the webpages of your website in a format that Google reads.

15) **Sitemap:** This is similar to an XML sitemap, except it is in a format that humans can read. This also helps with SEO, so be sure to add a sitemap to the footer area.

How easy is it?

Easy enough that someone like me with no website coding abilities can do it. It can be more of a grind than anything. But there are specific steps you need to follow. I'm going to show you exactly how I get websites ranked at the top for local searches. I'm going to break this down into 5 main steps, and then within those steps, I will walk you through the necessary pieces. Follow these steps with consistency and you will dominate the local searches!

Overview – 5 Steps to Dominate Google Searches with SEO

1) **Get a Google compliant website.** I covered some of this in strategy #4. But to dive deeper we need to optimize the on-page SEO, metadata, H1 title tags, alt tags, and sitemap.

2) **Get high quality, original keyword-rich content.** You've probably heard the phrase, "Content is King." That also applies to SEO. The goal is to have more quality content than your competitors.

3) **Get high authority back links.** This is the other main ingredient for SEO. You must have backlinks. The more high-quality websites that point to your website, the more Google feels your website must be an authority and they move you up in the rankings.

4) **Get a Google My Business Page.** This is a free page that Google provides for you to showcase your services and collect Google reviews.

5) **Get Google reviews.** I cover all of this Strategy #10 and I provide tips on how to get more reviews.

STEP 1 – Get a Google Compliant Website

Having a properly designed website is the basic foundation of on-page SEO. And on-page SEO is what starts you on the path to getting found online. **So it is critical that you get this right if you want your website to actually get found in Google searches.**

On-page SEO is comprised of three main areas:

1) Making sure your website has the right structure and is Google compliant.

2) Is optimized with correct H1 Titles, Meta Titles, Alt Tags, and Meta Descriptions.

3) Has the right keywords on your site (covered in step 2).

Let's take a closer look at on-page SEO and how to set it up on your website.

- **Make sure you build your website on WordPress.** It is the most flexible with regard to options for plugins, design, and speed. WordPress makes it easy to create your own content, pages, and blog, along with all of the details of Titles and Metadata.

- **Make sure your website is mobile-friendly.** When over 50% of Google searches are done on smartphones, your website better be mobile-friendly. Google will penalize your site if it is not. Check it here: https://search.google.com/test/mobile-friendly

- **Make sure it's fast.** The main page of your website and any sales pages should load fast. Ideally, you want your speed to be 4 seconds or less. Slow websites are penalized by Google, plus when you start advertising your costs can be higher. Check your speed here: https://gtmetrix.com and be sure to select 'Dallas' as your area if you're in the USA.

- **Make sure your site is secure and protected by SSL.** Not only does an insecure site look unprofessional, but it also makes buyers hesitant to hand their information to you. Google doesn't like non-secured sites. You want to be Google compliant so you can get found online, so make sure your site is secure.

- **Get good hosting.** Plan on spending $300 per year or more. The starter hosting packages that companies sell are okay if you don't want to get found on Google. But if you want your SEO to work, you need speed and you don't want to be on a server with tons of spam.

- **Use a Content Delivery Network (CDN).** I use Cloudflare. This basically speeds your website up. A CDN is fundamentally a geographically distributed group of servers that bounce your data off of their servers to speed up your website. A CDN is not the same as hosting, but a compliment to it. The great thing for local businesses is that it's free. Here's how it works: https://www.cloudflare.com/learning/cdn/what-is-a-cdn/

- **Title Tags:** What are title tags? I'm referring to your H1, H2, H3 Titles. When you build a webpage, whether it's a sales page, about me page, or a blog post, you start off by creating a Title for the page. This usually matches the URL slug because the slug is based on the Title you choose. You only want ONE H1 tag per page. This is what Google sees as the headline and relevancy of your page. All other Titles on the page should be H2, H3, etc. You can have multiple H2 titles, but only one H1 title. The lead title of your page or post should look like this:

Your H2 Title should look like this:

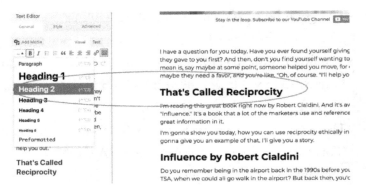

- **Alt Text:** This is the description you give your images, called Alternative Text. In Google, images are searchable as well. This is especially important if you sell products but should be done even if you just offer services. First, before you upload images, ensure the file is named appropriately. It should match what the picture is and what people search for. For example, a picture of a painter working, instead of the file being saved as IMG_2345.jpg, you should rename it to something like "Dallas-house-painter.jpg." This is indexed in Google and searchable. So when someone searches Dallas House Painter, and if they click on images, your image will show up and link to your website. You also want to ensure the Alt Text when you upload matches this. It should also say Dallas House Painter.

Here is an example taken from my website and how Alt Text is set up on the backend of your website builder when you add your images to your media folder.

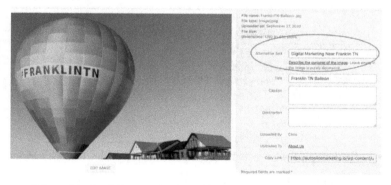

- **Meta Title:** This is the headline you see in the search results. Each page of your website will have one of these and they should each be unique. Do not make them all the same. Use a keyword you are trying to optimize for in the Meta Title, then you can add in your company name and phone number for your home pages or sales pages.

> **SEO Guarantee | Websites & Funnels | Autopil ot Marketing**
> https://autopilotmarketing.io/
> Explode your sales. Get ranked on page 1 of Google in 6 m onths or we work for FREE! Fast SEO. Website Design & F unnels. 866-615-1074

- **Meta Description:** This is the text below the headline. It is recommended to keep to just 166 characters because that's all that will display, but it's okay to go beyond that a little bit. It won't hurt your SEO. But you want to make sure to have your keywords in there. Make them flow naturally, don't just stuff them in there because Google will know and doesn't like that.

Here's an example:

> **SEO Guarantee | Websites & Funnels | Autopil ot Marketing**
> https://autopilotmarketing.io/
> Explode your sales. Get ranked on page 1 of Google in 6 m onths or we work for FREE! Fast SEO. Website Design & F unnels. 866-615-1074

- **Sitemap:** You want to make sure your website has 2 different types of sitemaps. I'm amazed at how many website designers skip this. If you want your website to be found on Google more easily, you need a sitemap. You want an HTML Sitemap and an XML Sitemap. Both are important. The HTML Sitemap is just a listing of all of your content. It should be a clickable link in the footer. This is where people can go to find a listing of all of your content. Google sees this and uses it as well. You also want an XML sitemap. This is the Sitemap that the Google spiders use to crawl and index your site. Both are important, but the XML Sitemap is a must. Most SEO plugins, like Yoast and SEO Press can do this for you automatically. Or just have your website developer install it.

Once you knock out these tasks, your website is nearly optimized for on-page SEO and is ready to start getting traffic and found on Google! Now we can start implementing the other 4 steps that power your SEO, starting with how to find and use the right keywords on your website.

STEP 2 – Get High Quality, Organic Keyword Content

You may have heard the saying 'Content is King.' With regard to websites and Google, it is still true. Google ranks websites for a lot of reasons, and nobody knows all of them. They use several hundred factors when determining how a website should rank, and they update or change these factors often.

What Google likes is to see content that keeps visitors to your site engaged and on your site longer. They like content that is useful and that visitors comment on. They like content that other websites link to because there is value in it.

These are the tasks you can take to win the content game and get your site ranking on page one.

TASK ONE: Do a Site Audit on Your Competitors

Google search your market. For example, if you are a commercial painter and you want to see who is on page one in your area, search "commercial painter Franklin TN." Now that you know who is winning the search game, we will see how many pages of content they have.

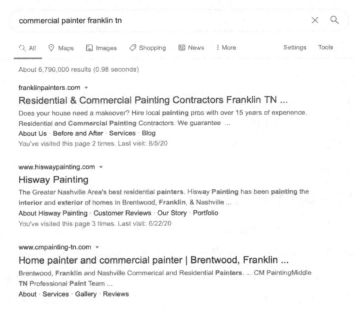

To see how much content your competitor has, type:

site:yourcompetitor'swebsite.com (see example below)

In this example, let's check the content of Hisway Painting. (They were number one before we started the process of getting my client to the #1 spot.)

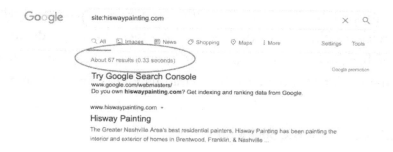

You can see here that Hisway Painting has 67 pages of content. So what we did was create more content than them.

TASK TWO: Create More Content Than Your Competitors

My client, franklinpainters.com is in the number one position for the search term in the example above. How did I get them there? Part of the process is content.

You want at least DOUBLE THE CONTENT of your competitors.

So we learned that the number one ranking website for the search term has 67 pages of content. So the goal would be to get 134 pages of content if you want to beat them out for this spot.

TASK THREE: Create Cornerstone Content

This would be a premier piece of content you have. For example, if you sold essential oils, you could create a very in-depth article that describes 101 uses for essential oils. Let's look at a case study.

Wellnessmama.com has an article on 101 uses for coconut oil. In that article, she describes the best uses, and links to her Amazon affiliate account where she promotes various products that use coconut oil, such as skin products and snacks. This article also is her cornerstone piece of content.

What that means is that as she continues to write other articles, she will reference this article with a link in all other articles, producing a lot of backlinks to that page. That cornerstone piece of content produces a lot of money for her via affiliate sales on Amazon and other places.

TASK FOUR: Write 500 Words

Google requires a minimum of 350 words on a page to index it for their search engine. Clay Clark in his excellent marketing book, *Search Engine Optimization Domination* recommends writing triple that at 1,000 words per page. That's a great recommendation and I concur. The reason might be because a lot of shorter blogs are 500 words, so doubling that content can help make yours more relevant in the eyes of Google. Google rewards websites that are engaging, shareable, and ones that keep people on the page longer.

But I've also found success with using content that is shorter. You just have to post content daily. The minimum word count you should shoot for is no less than 500 words.

TASK FIVE: Consistency

How often should you create content? EVERY DAY until you double the content of the competition. You want to consistently publish. **If you know you only need 134 pages of content and you create one article per day, you could be at the top in less than six months!**

Types of content: There are two main types of content used to boost SEO—Blogs and City Pages.

Blogs are articles you create that could be about anything related to your industry. They should be easy to read with useful information for your readers. And they should also be shareable. Create social sharing links on the blog post so people can easily share your content. You never know where it will land or who will read it!

City pages are pages of content that describe your products and services. The H1 title and URL slug should match the city. For example, I would create a page with the H1 title "Residential Painter in Franklin TN." The URL slug would be:

www.franklinpainters.com/residential-painter-franklin-tn

The page describes the company and services offered. Build out city pages for each of the local areas in your city that you serve. These are very powerful for getting higher rankings locally. You can also use these to build SEO in cities outside of your area if you are trying to expand.

How often should you create content?

Every Day!

Is there a better way?

No! You need content. Commit to doing this if you want to get ranked on Google.

Here Are Some Ways to Do It More Easily

Hire an agency.

We do this for clients who don't want to mess with creating content. But be sure the agency you hire offers a solid guarantee. We promise to get you ranked on page one in six months or we continue to work for free until we do.

Dictate the content.

If you don't enjoy writing, try dictating it by voice to convert to text. There are a few ways to do this and it can be much faster than typing. An article can be dictated in about 10 minutes.

- You can buy a dictation headset. It transcribes your words into text accurately.
- You can dictate into your phone and upload to rev.com. They will convert it to text for a couple of dollars. Then just upload it to your website. I personally use Rev.
- But the best method is to record a video and have rev.com transcribe the video to text. Next, upload the YouTube video to your blog. YouTube will help with your SEO. Then add the text that Rev converted for you to your blog post below your video. Now not only do you get the advantage of boosted SEO, but you offer your readers various mediums in which to consume your content. Some people prefer to read. Others prefer videos.

That's the simple version of getting started with creating lots of content. There are some other tricks like creating content around what's trending and what people are actively searching for. You can use Google Trends for this or just look at the bottom of the search results for your ideas to see what Google recommends for searches that are related to what you searched for.

Searches related to uses for coconut oil

how to use coconut oil **in cooking**	how to use coconut oil for **weight loss**
how to eat coconut oil	**beauty** uses for coconut oil
benefits of coconut oil **on skin**	**benefits of** coconut oil **on face**
coconut oil uses for **skin**	coconut oil **morning empty stomach**

STEP 3: Get High Authority Backlinks

Backlinks are just as important as content when it comes to SEO. Maybe even more so. This section will show you:

- Where to get backlinks.
- What not to do.
- How to spy on your competitors' backlinks.
- How often to get backlinks.

But first, let's refresh our memory on backlinks and how they help with SEO.

A backlink is when another website links to your website. The more authority a website linking to you has, the better it helps your website. These are called high authority backlinks. You can get these in several ways: citations, email outreach, and HARO.

Citations

Having a link to your website from places like Facebook, Yelp, Houzz, and the BBB would be considered citations.

These are fairly easy to set up. They just take a little time to create accounts, add company information, images, etc.

Email Outreach

The idea here is to reach out to a website blog that has a high volume of traffic (and is an authority) and ask them if you can write a blog for them. The key though would be to allow your profile to link back to your own website.

Another outreach strategy would be to write a high-quality blog for your website that covers areas that might be outdated or missing from a high-volume blog you found. You can email the owner of that site and show them that you have written a very in-depth article that their readers might like since it covers much more than the website they linked to their article originally.

HARO

HARO stands for Help A Reporter Out.

Reporters need experts and sources for their articles. If you are an expert in your field, reach out to HARO and be a source. They can refer to you and include links to your blogs, videos and website as proof.

Media Outlets Using HARO

1 MILLION SOURCES	75,000+ JOURNALISTS & BLOGGERS	THE MOST MEDIA OPPORTUNITIES

https://www.helpareporter.com

Press Releases

Press releases are not as high authority as citations or the other methods I mentioned above, but they do build backlinks to your website by publishing short articles about your business on digital news outlets like Google news.

A press release could be used when you open your business, when you add a new service, have a spring special, or hire a new employee.

There are ways to do this for free, or you can find places to publish it for you.

What Not to Do

As you can see there are a few great ways to get quality backlinks! **But one thing you definitely DO NOT want to do is to use Black Hat backlink strategies.** If you get caught Google will banish you to the bottom of the rankings, maybe to never return to the top again. Sadly, some SEO companies use black hat strategies, so be sure to ask what their methods are of building links to your website. **If they can't guarantee they don't use black hat, you are taking a big risk of losing your online presence.**

Some examples of black hat are keyword stuffing, buying links, and using Private Blog Networks.

Keyword stuffing is when you use the keyword you are trying to rank for unnaturally and too often. Here's an example, "Jake's Plumbing leads the area in emergency plumbing services. Our emergency plumbing services get great reviews. If you need emergency plumbing services call Jake's Plumbing."

You can see that the overuse of 'emergency plumbing services' seems unnatural. That's keyword stuffing, and Google does not like it and has technology to catch it—so don't do it!

Buying links is when you reach out to an authoritative website and offer to pay them for linking to your site. It can be harder to catch, but if caught, you'll have violated the Federal Trade Commission guidelines.

A common black hat strategy used is Private Blog Networks (PBNs). How this works is you would buy several old domains not in use that had a high volume of traffic. Recreate content similar to what was on the site, and then point those sites to your website with a redirect, essentially creating several high authority backlinks.

The problem is Google is getting smart at detecting this and if you are caught, you can kiss your rankings goodbye. Don't do this and do not hire an agency who uses this black hat strategy!

PBN Example

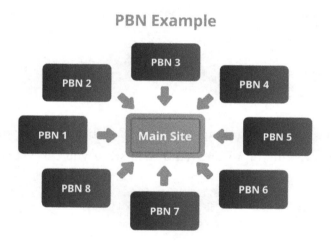

How to Spy on Your Competitors

This is something you should do . . . and it's easy. It's good to know what your competition is doing for backlinks and who is linking to them. There are several places to find out this information, but I like SEMrush.com

You can sign up for a free account. With the free account, you can get information on backlinks, keywords, and rankings.

If you were a dentist looking to get to the top of page one in Nashville, TN, you'd first Google "Dentist Nashville TN" to see who is at the top. Then plug that domain into SEMrush and click the Backlink Analytics button.

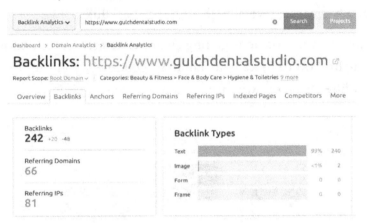

You can see the top-ranking dentist has 242 backlinks. Scroll down to see who is linking to them and then see if you can get the same backlinks.

This will show you exactly who is linking to them. Some of these will be citations that you can easily set up. Other backlinks might be from local news publications. And some could be from sites you never knew existed in your niche to help build authority.

It's a great resource and will give you instant information and ammunition to compete with the top-ranking websites.

How Often Should You Build Backlinks?

The answer is: it depends. Backlinks should be built slowly and naturally over time. **If you have a new website, you should not build 500–1,000 backlinks in your first month.** That could flag Google as if you bought those links. But if your website is established and already has hundreds of backlinks, then it's okay to build more per month.

For a new website, my recommendation is to limit 1 backlink per day, or a maximum of 30 per month. In a month or two, feel free to bump it up to 2 backlinks per day. Over time, you can increase this to 5 or more per day. Once you get into the range where you have 1,000+ backlinks built, there is no real limit to how many you can build in a month. **The main takeaway is to build your backlinks naturally over time and NEVER buy them . . . unless you want your rankings to take a nosedive.**

STEP 4 – Get a Google My Business Page

This is the secret weapon to getting found online in local searches. If you own a local business and don't yet have a Google My Business (GMB) page, you need to set one up immediately. Having a GMB is critical for your SEO.

85% of people who search for the location of a business do so with Google Maps. Without a GMB page, your business won't show up. But what if you have a service business that operates out of your house and you don't want to display that? Good news! GMB lets you hide that, and you can choose a service area.

What is a local search?

When someone searches for something on Google with the intention of finding something locally or near them. For example, if you searched for "emergency plumber Nashville TN," the results would look like this:

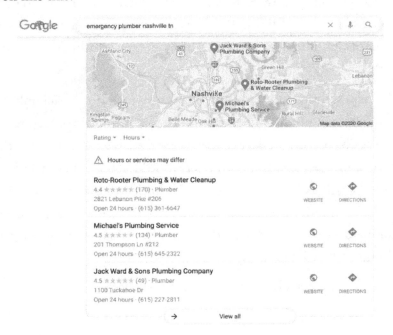

These search results are called the Local Pack. These listings are Google My Business pages. They include the Business name, address (if not hidden), reviews, a link to your website, and directions.

You can see how powerful these are for attracting new clients. The odds of someone clicking over to page 2 versus looking at one of these 3 companies is not very high.

You can also use a term like "coffee near me." Google will take your location into account and show you the results relevant to your search. **So the next question is, how do you get your company in the local pack?**

Google Local Listings

The good news is that Google tells you exactly how they determine who gets visibility on the local pack.

Relevance: How closely does your business match with what the person is searching for?

Distance: How far away is your business from the current location of the person or the city entry the person typed in?

Prominence: How well-known is your business?

Before I go into detail about how these three areas work, you need to first set up and claim your GMB page.

Setting up Your Google My Business page

Start with signing up for your free GMB account:

https://www.google.com/business/

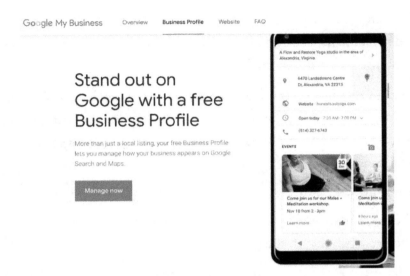

When you log in, you will set up your account and Google will ask you to verify your business identity with a pin code. This can be done via email, text, or a postcard to the business address. It's important to not skip this step because this is the part of claiming ownership of your page.

Essentially, anyone can set up a GMB page, and they could set one up under your business name. **But the accounts that have been verified rank higher and can only be edited and managed by the person who verified it.** So don't skip this step!

Once you've done that, it's time to start adding in your company information.

- Business name
- Category
- Hours of operation
- Address (you can also hide this and choose service area—I recommend this for home-based businesses)

- Photos of your business, projects, or products
- Phone number
- Website URL

Relevance

The more detailed your listing is, the more relevant it can be. If Google doesn't have a lot of information, it will be hard for it to decide to display your GMB page. Things like having your business listed in the proper category would matter. Photos should have accurate descriptions, and the file name should not be IMG_234.jpg. Be sure to change the image file name before uploading to Google. All of that is searchable.

Attributes are another important factor in relevance. Think of these as tags for your business. If you owned a restaurant, your attributes would be things like this:

- Outdoor seating
- Rooftop bar
- Italian cuisine
- Family-friendly
- Free WIFI

Google also creates their own attributes on your business as you collect reviews or are mentioned elsewhere on the internet, such as:

- Good for kids
- Popular for lunch
- Cozy atmosphere

Distance

This ranking factor is fairly easy to understand. Google uses what you type and your GPS location to determine the best places closest to you.

Search results can be from what you type, "coffee shop on Main Street" or the location data from your phone.

There is one caveat though. **Relevance trumps Distance.** If Google feels a business is more relevant, even though it is further away, it will rank that one higher in the local pack.

Prominence

The more well-known and popular your business is online, the higher it will rank. How does Google determine this? Basically, it comes down to the strength of your brand. Your website site plays a large part in branding.

Often the bigger brands get more clicks and more reviews, all of which make the brand more prominent. For you to compete against the bigger brands, it starts with getting a properly designed website and getting it ranked in Google.

For example, if your website ranks well in Google searches, Google sees your website as an authority in your business category and that will help rank you higher in the local pack.

Now let's talk about the power of customer reviews for your Google My Business listing. Not only do they help you build authority, but they help with SEO.

STEP 5 – Get Google Customer Reviews

Once your GMB page is set up, it's time to start getting reviews. Google reviews are a very powerful marketing tool. And what you may not know is that Google reviews help power your SEO.

Reviews can boost your website SEO by about 10%. And the more reviews you have, the better it helps your rankings for local Google searches.

You can display your reviews right on your website as well. And even hide anything less than 4 stars if you want.

Your strategy for getting reviews will be different depending on the type of business you are in. For example, if you own a home improvement company, you'll want to wait a week or so after the work is complete to ask for a review. Let your client enjoy the work you did.

If you help people get results, you can probably ask for a review right after you've gotten those results for them. If you own a gym or yoga studio, the time frame might be a month before you are ready to ask for reviews.

To send a link to get a Google review, log in to your GMB page. You will see the link on the right side of the page. Just click the "share review form" button and it will generate the link to send.

Your main takeaway should be: Get More Reviews! I go into more detail on how to do this easier and faster in Strategy #10.

STRATEGY #9: FOLLOW UP

When I ask most business owners what they think of when I mention follow up for prospects who inquire about their services or products, they think of sales calls. While that may work in some businesses, I want you to think differently about this.

I'm referring to a missed opportunity.

Most prospects, even if they are looking for your service aren't ready to buy just yet. **They are just in research mode.**

Here's a study that breaks down buyer readiness and willingness to buy.

Of the people who contact you for information (whether through your website, a phone call, direct mail, or opting in for your free information):

- 50% will not buy from anyone. For whatever reason, they aren't ready or never were.
- 50% will buy from someone.
- Of the 50% who are interested:
- 3% ready to buy immediately.
- 12% ready to buy in 0–90 days.
- 85% won't buy for up to 18 months.

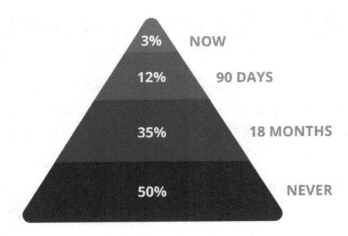

BUYER READINESS

The 15% are your hot buyers. We target them with Google Ads (and Direct Mail can work also). But Google is magic because they are searching online to solve an urgent problem. Remember this from Strategy #1, getting clarity?

When they search on Google and see your catchy headline and amazing offer, you have better odds of capturing that client. We can also target this 15% with social media and Facebook retargeting.

But what about the 85%? **This is a huge opportunity to get a lot more business,** and HARDLY ANY local businesses have any way to contact someone who visited their site for information. They may have liked what you said and offered, but time goes by, we get busy, and they forget about you. **You want to bring them into your world so they can get to know you and your business on a deeper level.**

To do this, you need to capture their contact information: email and/or phone number so that you can follow up with them at a later date. This needs to be done strategically.

The process starts with offering something of value first (usually for free) to get their email or phone number. This will allow you to do several things.

First, by giving something away of value for free, you harness the power of reciprocity and make your business more likable. They will feel more inclined to buy from you versus the competition that does not offer this. This could be a free guide, book, or training video. And because the information is likely educational, you also position your company as an authority in your industry and niche. You can also use coupons, but I prefer offering something educational because it puts you on a pedestal compared to the company using coupons.

Secondly, by getting their contact information, you are able to email, text, or call them—depending on your market. But email or text messages are the preferred methods. Personally, I like email. Even though we all get a lot of email, if you offer high-value emails, yours will have a greater chance of being opened.

You should be using an email autoresponder that sends emails automatically after someone subscribes. You want to use an email sequence, or a series of emails to send them what they signed up for and to stay in touch with them.

The Email Sequence

Day 1. What you want to do is immediately email them the download with a very short intro on what they are going to get from the thing that they just opted in for. Even if it's a coupon, tell them what they get and why it's so awesome.

Day 2. Email them with a story. You can use a story about you, your company, or a client. This story should closely match what it is you are trying to sell and the offer that they opted in for. For example, if you are a dog trainer, and you had a free guide on "5 Easy Steps to Stop Your Dog from Peeing in The House," you would want to tell a story about how you helped a client with their dog.

Day 3. This is a good time to reintroduce yourself. Tell your story in an email. People connect with stories. We love stories.

These first 3 emails should not have any sales copy or you trying to sell them on something. You're just doing brand awareness and slowly building a relationship.

Day 4 is where you have an offer. You may want to remind them of why they came to you in the first place and downloaded your free information. You could start off by asking if they are enjoying the information guide. Are they getting value? Then you can tell them that if they want more, you have this amazing offer. This a good place to use scarcity. Let them know it is for a limited time or quantity.

Remembering back to scarcity and buyer psychology, people like to procrastinate. They need motivation to push them over the line. Send the offer to a landing page with your irresistible offer, sales copy, and testimonials.

Then you just continue to send weekly emails and newsletters. Keep your company on their mind, even if it's in the back of their mind, that's okay. Because in 9 months or a year when they are ready, your business will be one of the first they think of and reach out to.

The 9-Word Email

Another method to use email and follow up is by using the 9-word email. I learned this from Dean Graziosi, but I believe it was first created by Dean Jackson. How it works is like this . . .

After they opt-in to your email list for your free information, you would send them the guide. Then you would follow up with a very short and simple email that literally has 9 words (it can be slightly longer but keep it to one sentence).

Let's continue using the example of the dog trainer and the prospect who downloaded the "5 Easy Steps to Stop Your Dog from Peeing in The House."

Your 9-word email should have the prospect's name in the title "John."

The content of the email would be simple and short:

"Hi John,

How often is your dog having accidents in your house?

Chris"

The cool thing about this type of email is that it is conversational. You are engaging with your prospect just like you would if they came into your place of business and told you about their problem. So think of what would be the next likely question you could ask them that they would be willing to respond to?

This 9-word email can be set up to go out automatically. But because of how you word it, it appears to be sent manually. Once they respond, you can reply manually, engage in a conversation, direct them to your offers, or set up a consultation.

If your free guide was a little more general, like "5 Tips for a Well-Behaved Dog," your 9-word email might ask, "What behavior challenges are you having with your dog?"

So there are two excellent methods of using follow up that you can use to continue the conversation you started with your prospect and to keep your business brand in front of them.

STRATEGY #10: GET REVIEWS

When it comes to marketing, there's hardly anything more powerful than a personal referral or recommendation. When someone is looking for a service you offer, they will likely ask friends and family first to see if they can recommend anyone. Personal recommendations have a high value.

But even so, unless I completely trust that person's judgment, I will do a little more research myself. I'll Google their business to see what kind of reviews they get. I might also check them out on Facebook, but I think you'll find a lot of people defer to googling a business.

Many people will just search for your business and give reviews without you asking. That can be good and bad and really depends upon how well you run your business. Do you offer a 5-star experience or a 1-star experience?

It should be pretty obvious, but if you want 5-star reviews, you need to deliver a 5-star experience. I recommend starting with the experience you'd have to give to get 5 stars, and then work backwards from there. Define and redefine all of the touchpoints with your customer along the way.

Five-star reviews do a couple of things for your business. It acts like both a drawbridge and a moat around a castle.

Hundreds of reviews act like a moat. It's hard for competitors to compete when you dominate in this area.

Reviews also act like a drawbridge. They allow prospects to see what others like them think of your business, products, and service. There's serious power in reviews.

There are a few ways to use this:

- Testimonials on your website (least effective)
- Google reviews (effective and helps with SEO)
- And video reviews (most effective)

I'm not going to cover testimonials here because I really don't think that they are all that powerful anymore, at least not when you stack them up against Google reviews and video reviews.

Google Reviews

Here are some tips to get more positive reviews for your business:

1) Just ask your most recent and best clients if they'd be willing to give you a very quick online review. Be honest with them and tell them that you are trying to build up your reviews. If they agree, email or text them a link to your review page.

2) To really boost and build up your reviews, you're going to make an offer to your current customers.

- First, compile a list of your best clients. These are the ones you know are your biggest fans and would likely leave you a great review.
- Second, create an irresistible offer that is very low cost to you out of pocket but of value to your customers.
- Third, tell them that if they can give you an honest Google review, they will receive that irresistible offer for

free. But they must act soon. Give them a date where if they don't complete the review, they don't get the offer. I'd recommend 3–5 days. (A word of caution: do not ask them for a good review or 5-star review. It must be done ethically. You are simply asking for an honest review, which is why you want to ask your best clients).

I learned about this technique in Amy Porterfield's podcast. The business owner, who used tip number 2, owned a dance studio for girls in Wisconsin. She offered a free pair of girls' dance tights to the moms in exchange for a Google review. She got 50+ reviews in a few days. It was an offer that didn't cost her a lot out of pocket and something the dance moms were willing to spend 5 minutes writing a review to get.

What would fifty 5-star reviews do for your business?

Video Reviews

When it comes to reviews online, having video testimonials on your website are pretty convincing. These are your case studies. Stories from your clients who you've helped.

Imagine getting a personal recommendation from someone for a dog trainer. Then, you do a quick Google search and see they have fifty 5-star Google reviews. Then after visiting their website, you see they have quite a few video testimonials from past clients telling what a great experience it was working with you and the incredible results you provided.

If you weren't convinced before, after watching a slew of positive video reviews from real clients, the odds go up that you'll call them. This is the power of video.

Video is rawer and more authentic than almost anything else. When almost nothing is real these days, news articles, primetime news, and even reality TV, people crave authenticity. Video reviews provide that—especially when you have several of them.

How to Get Video Reviews

The easiest way is to just ask your client for one. Tell them it's informal and that you'll just ask them a quick few questions about their experience. Pull out your phone, and video a selfie with you and your client.

Use the same technique we did with getting more GMB reviews, which is to email them a link to record a video. But with this, give them specific instructions. Reviews should be no more than 2 minutes. A pro tip is to lay out a specific script outline.

The script might go like this: 1) Have them tell the viewers who they are. 2) What their BIG problem was. 3) Optional—an issue they've had in the past with other companies. 4) What they bought from you. 5) How it changed their life, made it easier, saved them money, etc.

Here are some online tools for getting video reviews:

- www.videopeel.com
- www.boast.io
- www.magnfi.com

A quick note about video reviews. **Most important is the audio quality.** Be sure there is minimal background noise. If you are recording reviews yourself, try using a microphone that plugs into your iPhone for better audio quality. Test the audio before you shoot the video. You can also use a separate audio recording device in addition to your phone to be sure to capture the audio. You can always sync up with the video later in editing if needed.

If sending a link for your customers to record a video for you on their own, **give clear instructions for audio quality.** They don't need a microphone to record their video. Just give them instructions to find a quiet place to record with no wind.

Lastly, the video does not need to be long. Video testimonials don't need to be more than 1–3 minutes in length, and I'd suggest 5 minutes should be the maximum. Once you start getting into longer videos, those would be considered more of an in-depth case study and you'd use those in your sales funnels for your product launches.

CONCLUSION

Awesome! Now you know 1,000% more than 99% of local business owners. Your next job is to take massive action and put these 10 strategies in place. Just imagine where your business will be in 6 months when you do. But what happens if you continue to do what you've been doing? You'll keep getting more of what you've always gotten.

So take action! **You can do this.** If you go through these 10 strategies one-by-one, you'll nail them down and before you know it, you'll have exploded your sales and maybe even doubled your revenue in 6 months.

The key is to get momentum. That starts with commitment on your part. You need to mentally commit to this.

There are three ways that you can achieve this success:

1. Hire us! At Autopilot Marketing, we can strategize with you one-on-one to get your business rocking. We start with listening, consulting, evaluating your goals, website, offers, competition, and Google rankings. Then we implement the strategies listed in this playbook for you. We also guarantee page one SEO rankings in 6 months or we work for free—an irresistible offer in and of itself.

2. Go through our comprehensive online course, the Autopilot Marketing System, www.autopilotmarketing.io/system, for a fraction of the price of having our agency do everything for you. This course is self-paced, works on mobile devices, and

teaches everything we do to get your digital marketing in tip-top shape and explode your leads and sales faster!

3. Take this information and hire someone else. Of course, I would be remiss if I didn't try to win your business. I truly feel we have the best service on the planet, but should you want to go somewhere else, you have our 10 strategies as a guide when you hire your agency!

At the end of the day, I hope you gained great insight into why effective marketing is so important to a business. And I hope you also feel excited and ready to attack this and totally explode your business!

Now, Go Be Awesome!

Chris Loomis

ACKNOWLEDGEMENTS

To my editor Johanna Petronella Leigh, who not only had thoughtful edits while protecting my writing voice, but also made me sound much smarter than I am. Thank you.

To my mentors who paved the way: Jeff Walker, Dean Graziosi, Tony Robbins, Russell Brunson, Dan Kennedy, Joe Polish, Dean Jackson, Jim Edwards, Mike Dillard, and Jordon Mederich. You are geniuses.

To my grandmother Patricia for being my number one fan. You're the best.

And to my wife Amy. You have never wavered in your support of my ambitions and have followed me to what feels like the ends of the earth and back. I love you.

RECOMMENDED READINGS & REFERENCES

Do you want more knowledge? Then check out the references from this book. These are all great books and podcast episodes that you might enjoy and can definitely benefit from. Study these along with what I have written in this book and you will go to another level with your marketing skills.

- Brunson, Russell. (2017) *Expert Secrets: The Underground Playbook for Creating a Mass Movement of People who will Pay for your Advice.*
- Cialdini, Robert. (1984) *Influence: The Psychology of Persuasion.*
- Clay, Bruce. (2015) *Search Engine Optimization All-in-one for Dummies, 3Rd Edition.*
- Edwards, Jim. (2018) *Copywriting Secrets: How Everyone Can Use The Power Of Words To Get More Clicks, Sales, and Profits…No Matter What You Sell Or Who You Sell It To!*
- Graziosi, Dean. (2017) *Millionaire Success Habits.*
- Kelly, Jonathan & Clark, Clay. (2019) *Search Engine Domination: The Proven Plan, Best Practice Processes, & Super Moves to Make Millions with Online Marketing.*
- Kennedy, Dan. (2018) *Magnetic Marketing.*

- Polish, Joe & Jackson, Dean. *Breakthrough DNA – 8 Profit Activators You Can Trigger in Your Business Right Now.* Retrieved from URL https://ilovemarketing.com/breakthrough/
- Porterfield, Amy with Tuschl, Stacy. (2020) *Take Your Brick & Mortar Business Online.* "Online Marketing Made Easy" a podcast by Amy Porterfield. Retrieved from URL https://www.amyporterfield.com/2020/04/310/
- Reeves, Rosser. (1960) *Reality in Advertising.*
- Robbins, Tony with Abraham, Jay. *World Class Marketing, Strategic Innovation, and How to Grow a Business Exponentially.* The Tony Robbins Podcast. Retrieved from URL https://www.tonyrobbins.com/podcasts/vault-tony-robbins-jay-abraham-part-1/ & https://www.tonyrobbins.com/podcasts/vault-tony-robbins-jay-abraham-part-2/

CPSIA information can be obtained
at www.ICGtesting.com
Printed in the USA
LVHW021143210121
676969LV00006B/673